HEROES OF HISTORY

WILLIAM WILBERFORCE

Take Up the Fight

HEROES OF HISTORY

WILLIAM WILBERFORCE

Take Up the Fight

JANET & GEOFF BENGE

Emerald Books

P.O. BOX 635, LYNNWOOD, WA 98046

Emerald Books are distributed through YWAM Publishing. For a full list of titles, including other great biographies, visit our website at www.emeraldbooks.com.

William Wilberforce: Take Up the Fight

Published by Emerald Books
P.O. Box 635
Lynnwood, WA 98046

Library of Congress Cataloging-in-Publication Data
Benge, Janet, 1958–
William Wilberforce : take up the fight / Janet and Geoff Benge.
pages cm. — (Heroes of history)
Includes bibliographical references.
Summary: "Narrative biography of William Wilberforce, English member of Parliament, social reformer, and abolitionist who worked for decades to abolish slavery in the British Empire"—Provided by publisher.
ISBN 978-1-62486-057-7 (pbk.)—ISBN 978-1-62486-070-6 (e-book)
1. Wilberforce, William, 1759–1833—Juvenile literature. 2. Legislators—Great Britain—Biography—Juvenile literature. 3. Abolitionists—Great Britain—Biography—Juvenile literature. 4. Philanthropists—Great Britain—Biography—Juvenile literature. 5. Great Britain—Politics and government—1760–1820—Juvenile literature. 6. Great Britain—Politics and government—1820–1830—Juvenile literature. I. Benge, Geoff, 1954– II. Title.
DA522.W6B47 2015
326.092—dc23
[B] 2015010610

Third Printing 2025

ISBN 978-162486-057-7 (paperback)
ISBN 978-162486-070-6 (e-book)

Printed in the United States of America

HEROES OF HISTORY

Abraham Lincoln
Alan Shepard
Ben Carson
Benjamin Franklin
Benjamin Rush
Billy Graham
Captain John Smith
Christopher Columbus
Clara Barton
Davy Crockett
Daniel Boone
Douglas MacArthur
Dwight Eisenhower
Elizabeth Fry
Ernest Shackleton
Frederick Douglass
George Washington
George Washington Carver
Harriet Tubman
John Adams
Laura Ingalls Wilder
Louis Zamperini
Meriwether Lewis
Milton Hershey
Orville Wright
Ronald Reagan
Theodore Roosevelt
Thomas Edison
William Bradford
William Penn
William Wilberforce
Winston Churchill

Available in paperback, e-book, and audiobook formats.
Curriculum Guides are available for all of the U.S. biographies.
www.Heroesofhistory.com

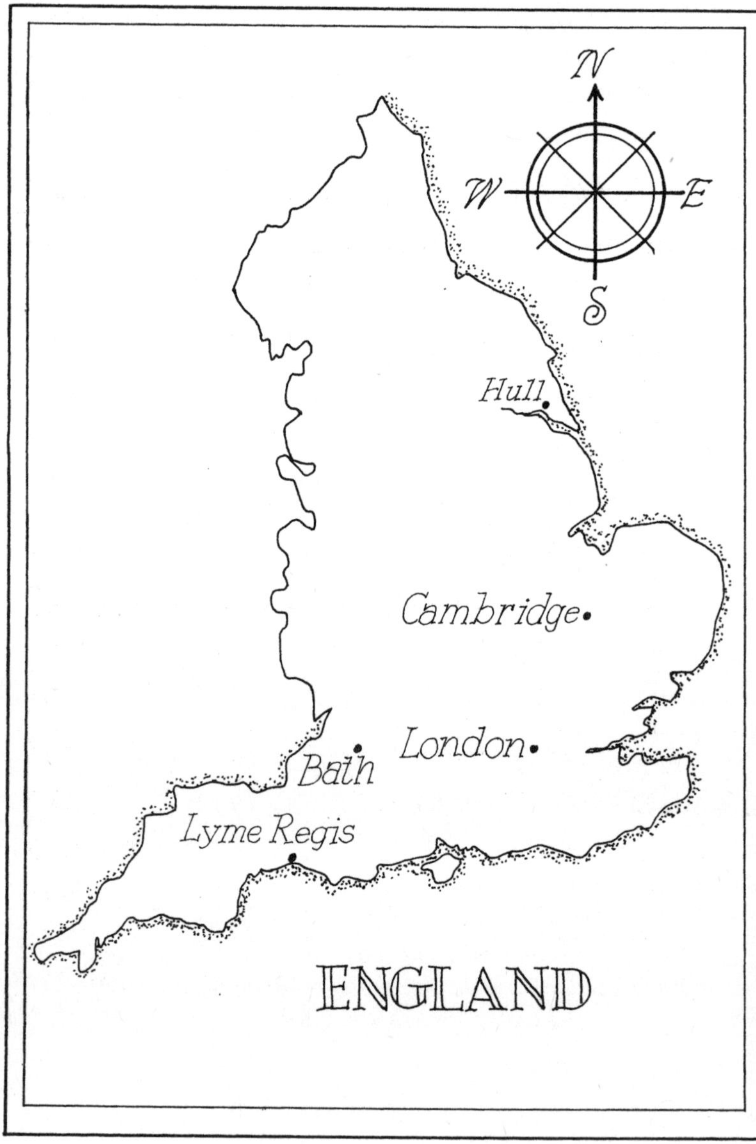
N
W
E
S
Hull
Cambridge
London
Bath
Lyme Regis
ENGLAND

Contents

Chapter 1

Turmoil

William Wilberforce walked along the river wall behind his house on High Street. He shielded his eyes from the sun and stared down at the muddy Hull River looking for ships flying his family's crest. The black eagle of the crest was distinctive. In the distance William could spot the flag on ships sailing up the Humber River before they rounded the spit and came up the Hull River. His father had told him that the Wilberforce Company was expecting a ship filled with timber from Norway and iron and tar from Sweden to arrive today from the Baltic region.

The day before, William had watched dockworkers load bales of Yorkshire wool and bolts of sailcloth into the company warehouse beside the river at the back of the Wilberforce home. Once the cargo had been unloaded from the ship, huge nets were used to hoist a new cargo from the other end of the warehouse onto the ship for the return voyage. William enjoyed most watching the Yorkshire ponies, usually bound for Russia, being loaded. A sling was wrapped around each pony, and one by one, the kicking and wriggling animals were hoisted aboard by a wood-framed crane. No matter how many times William watched a ship sail up the river, dock beside the warehouse, and unload and reload cargo, he never got bored. There was so much to see.

Hull was the fourth largest port in England, after London, Bristol, and Liverpool. William's ancestors, the Wilberforces and the Thorntons, had been merchants for over a hundred years, and William was sure that his father, Robert, knew all there was to know about trading with Europe. Much of his information came from the captains of ships who often came to the house for dinner. William listened to the business talk as the men ate, but most of all he loved to hear about shipwrecks and pirates. His sister Sarah, or Sally, as everyone called her, loved to hear these stories too. Sally was a year older than William, and the captains often brought the two of them chocolates from Holland, along with tulips for their mother's garden and port wine for their father.

Until a month ago, William had had another sister. Fourteen-year-old Elizabeth had been at boarding school in London when she suddenly fell ill and died. A messenger had arrived at the house with the news, and Robert Wilberforce immediately galloped off to London to escort his daughter's body back to be buried at Holy Trinity Church. William and Sally were dressed in black mourning clothes—black stockings, jacket, and cap for William, and a black matte silk dress, crepe hat, and veil for Sally.

William and Sally were expected to stay indoors for days. William's mother never left the house after receiving the news of Elizabeth's death. She was normally the hub of various social gatherings in the community—card evenings, plays, dinner parties, and the other things the upper-class residents of Hull did to entertain themselves. But now she stayed in her bedroom. William knew that her behavior change was partly due to Elizabeth's death and partly because she was eight months pregnant. He hoped that the new baby would be a boy, a little brother for him to play with. Even though the baby would be nine years younger, William still imagined himself teaching his new brother to play marbles and walk safely along the top of the river wall.

Walking along the wall was one of William's favorite pastimes. With the wind blowing through his hair and the sound of the gulls overhead, William could let his imagination run wild. Sometimes he was a cabin boy on his way to France, while at other times he was a burly whaler setting sail for Greenland. On Saturdays, when school was out, William often walked along the wall, past the Peases' warehouse and the Blaydeses' home, past the shipbuilding docks, and out into the country. He loved the countryside almost as much as the river. He would sit for a long time listening to the croaking toads and watching them leap into ponds and swim around. Sometimes he would spot a badger foraging among the trees for worms and insects. William's teachers at Hull Grammar School, Master Joseph Milner and his brother, Master Isaac Milner, encouraged William to keep a nature diary, which was always tucked inside his waistcoat.

The Milner brothers were both excellent teachers. William's grandfather, whom William was named after, had served as Hull's mayor and was a longstanding alderman. He had handpicked Joseph Milner to be the schoolmaster when William was old enough to start attending school at seven years of age. Joseph Milner had won the Chancellor's Medal at Cambridge and had been the curate at North Ferriby, where Grandfather Wilberforce lived. Joseph's eighteen-year-old brother, Isaac, was his assistant. To William, Isaac looked like a giant, but a gentle one, and Isaac knew how to make mathematics interesting.

Unlike many other boys his age, William loved school. On his walks, he often thought about school. It was a wonderful place. He knew he probably got special attention from the Milners because his father was one of the wealthiest men in Hull, but William also thought that the brothers genuinely liked him. He was often singled out to read to the class. At nine years of age, William was small—smaller than most of the new entrants, who were seven years old—and he had poor eyesight, but he had a powerful voice. Joseph Milner would lift William onto the top of a desk and ask him to read passages from Shakespeare. William loved the sound of the words as he read.

One Saturday when William returned from his walk in the countryside, he found the house filled with activity. The baby was coming! Aunt Mary, William's mother's sister who was married to William's father's business partner, Abel Smith, was instructing the cook to boil water and the maid to bring clean linens and towels. William and Sally played a game of chess in the drawing room waiting for news.

The baby came soon enough. William and Sally now had a new sister named Anne, and not the brother William had hoped for. The children were allowed to tiptoe into their mother's bedroom, the same room William had been born in, to see the newly arrived tiny pink bundle. There was celebrating in the Wilberforce home. William's father handed out bottles of Madeira to the clerks who worked in the counting house and gave each household servant a shiny new shilling.

The celebration of the birth of the new baby soon turned to shock, however, as William's father fell seriously ill. In just a matter of days, Robert Wilberforce died. The family was thrown into turmoil. William, who had hardly adjusted to the idea that his sister Elizabeth was buried in the local church graveyard, watched his father's body being lowered into the grave at St. Mary's Church in Beverly, where the Wilberforces hailed from originally and where William's great-grandparents were buried. It was almost too much to bear. With her husband gone, William's mother seldom came downstairs, and a nursemaid looked after baby Anne. The house felt empty to William.

Uncle Abel Smith, who lived in Nottinghamshire, took over the family business, renaming it Wilberforce and Smith. He left most of the day-to-day dealings of the company in the hands of Thomas Thompson, who had been Robert Wilberforce's right-hand man.

Less than a year later, the Wilberforce family encountered a new crisis. This time it was William's mother who was seriously ill. A family conference was called. William was not allowed to attend, but he overheard snippets of conversation between his grandfather and his aunts and uncles. From what William could gather, his mother wanted to send him away to school and wanted someone else to take responsibility for him in case she died.

William's mind whirled with possibilities. His family was complicated. He could hardly keep the connections straight. His father had an older brother, also named William, and two sisters, Judith and Anne. Uncle William and his wife, Hannah, who was also William's father's first cousin, lived in London. Aunt Judith was married to John Bird, who was William's mother's brother, while Aunt Anne was married to John Greathed. All of these relatives were also merchants or bankers. Eventually the family conference decided that William should go to London to live with Uncle William and Aunt Hannah. The couple had no children of their own and said they would welcome William with open arms.

In summer 1769, Uncle William came to Hull to take his nephew back to London. On the way to London they stopped at Wilford House in Nottinghamshire, where Uncle Abel and Aunt Mary Smith lived. Sadly, the Smiths' oldest son and William's cousin, Thomas, had just died, and the Smith family was in mourning.

William had just celebrated his tenth birthday on August 24, 1769. As he climbed into the coach in Nottinghamshire for the trip to London to begin a new life, he felt much older than his years. The coach trip to London was long, bumpy, and dangerous. At night they would lodge at inns along the way. During the day as they headed south, the coach driver and even Uncle William were constantly on the lookout for highwaymen wanting to rob them. William didn't know much about London. He'd never been there, though he did know that it was huge, with over three quarters of a million people, none of whom he knew, living the city.

Once he arrived in London, William soon learned that he had a knack for making friends with all sorts of people. And he was curious about everything around him. His aunt and uncle had two beautiful homes. One was a villa in the countryside at Wimbledon, called Lauriston House, which had three acres of manicured lawns and gardens for William to roam in. At Lauriston House, William soon got to know the gardener and learned how to prune apple trees and store bulbs for spring. Uncle William had commissioned a famous artist named Angelica Kauffman to paint stunning murals inside the house on the walls of the staircase and on the ceilings.

The other house was in the center of London activity at St. James's Place. King George III had a house nearby, as did many of the richest men in England. Uncle William was certainly one of them. He was one of the biggest merchants in London, trading with merchants in Europe, just as William's own father had done.

Although William loved both houses, he did not spend much time in them. He was shipped off to boarding school in Putney, outside London. William was disappointed by this, but he soon settled into the routine of school, learning writing, French, math, and Latin. William's new schoolmaster didn't know how to make the lessons interesting in the way that the Milner brothers had back in Hull. William also found the food served at the school greasy and hard to keep down. He longed for the delicious meals the family cook in Hull had made him.

If the school in Putney didn't suit William, holidays and long weekends with Aunt Hannah and Uncle William did. Since the couple had no children, William fit into their family like a longed-for son. The Wilberforces took him everywhere and introduced him to their friends. It was eye-opening for William, who met the most interesting people in London, some of whom would change the course of his life.

Chapter 2

A New Life

William soon learned that his uncle's and aunt's lives revolved around their Methodist faith. He'd never met a Methodist before, and his mother had often warned against them. She told him that all Methodists were poor, uneducated fanatics who would never amount to anything. That certainly did not describe Uncle William or Aunt Hannah Wilberforce, or the Thornton family.

Since he liked to get to the bottom of things, William asked his uncle what a Methodist really was. Uncle William explained that a Methodist was a person who belonged to one of the Methodist Societies started by John Wesley, an Anglican clergyman. The societies stressed living a life of Christian holiness, which meant loving God with all your heart, mind, soul, and strength and loving your neighbor as yourself. The societies also provided guidance to members on how to go about doing this day to day. Uncle William stressed that members of the Methodist Societies were still active members of the Church of England. William was sure that his mother had not known any of this when she sent him to live in London with his uncle and aunt.

Uncle William and Aunt Hannah spent a lot of time in the company of John and Lucy Thornton. John was Aunt Hannah's half brother and also William's and Uncle William's cousin. He too was a rich man. The Thorntons had three sons, Samuel, Robert, and Henry, and a daughter, Jane. William especially loved it when Henry came to visit with his father. Henry was six months younger than William, and the two boys loved exploring the garden at Lauriston House and walking down to the Thames River to watch the ships sail by from the house at St. James's Place.

During school vacations, the Thorntons took William to many Christian meetings. The ones William loved most were at the Church of St. Peter and St. Paul in Olney, about sixty miles north of London. William especially liked these meetings because he got to hear the curate preach. The curate was a big, plainspoken man named John Newton, who was about the same age as Uncle William. When the Reverend Newton preached, he sounded like he had led a hundred lives. The Reverend Robinson, the vicar back at Holy Trinity Church in Hull, was very hard to follow when he preached. He used a lot of "thees" and "thous" in his sermons, and most of the time William could not understand his point. Not that that had bothered anyone in William's family. As respectable members of Hull society, William's parents rented a pew and gave toward the fund for the poor and destitute in the parish, but neither of them had been enthusiastic Christians. It was quite the opposite. His mother, in particular, thought that paying too much attention to religion was the road to ruin.

John Newton was everything the vicar at Hull was not. He often talked about his own life and how he had been a terrible sinner before becoming a Christian. One Sunday William was struck by his sermon on Jonah. The Reverend Newton read from the Bible about how Jonah, the central character in the book of Jonah, was commanded by God to go to the city of Nineveh. Jonah decided to sail to Tarshish instead. Along the way a huge storm arose. Jonah admitted to the sailors that he had displeased God, and to save themselves, they threw him overboard. Newton related how he had once been aboard a ship sailing off the west coast of Africa. At the time he was not a Christian and had caused so much trouble on board that the captain threatened to throw him overboard, just as in the story of Jonah. Listening to John Newton was better than any adventure story William had ever read.

In June 1771, John Newton invited the Wilberforce family to stay in the house next to the rectory in Olney. During the visit, the Reverend Newton spent many hours talking with William and allowing him to ask whatever questions he wanted. William soon discovered that the two of them were alike in some ways: John Newton's mother had died when John was seven, and John had been sent away to boarding school. His father was a sea captain, and when John turned eleven, the same age as William, his father took him to sea with him aboard ship. John loved life at sea until one day when he was kidnapped and forced to board a British naval vessel. The word for this, he told William, was *impressment*. He had been "impressed" into His Majesty's navy on a warship helping to fend off French ships attempting to attack England.

John Newton also told William how he had sailed to Africa and witnessed many troubling things in the slave trade. He'd even been a slave himself! In Africa he had partnered with a ship's captain who turned on him, took him prisoner, and gave him away as a slave. John was treated so poorly that he feared he might starve to death before his father sent someone to find him and buy his freedom.

All this astonished William, who wasn't used to listening to such colorful characters, yet he soon learned to trust John Newton like a father. John encouraged William in the Christian faith, admonishing him to follow in his uncle William's footsteps and the practices of the Methodists.

William began reading his Bible every night before he went to sleep and prayed for his mother, who was recovering from her serious illness, and his sisters, Sally and Anne. He also prayed that he might learn how to love God the way John Newton and his aunt and uncle did.

While William was enthralled with John Newton, Uncle William and Aunt Hannah spoke often of another great clergyman they knew. George Whitefield had spent many years preaching in the American colonies and left London in 1769, just before William moved there, for his sixth visit to America. Sadly, he died in America on September 30, 1770, but William still remembered how excited Uncle William and Aunt Hannah were whenever they received a letter from him. They would read every word of Whitefield's letter and then pass the letter on to their friends to read. Each letter was also read aloud at many meetings. William enjoyed hearing the letters being read. They contained all sorts of interesting pieces of information about life in the American colonies, as well as encouragement to the Methodists in London.

Whitefield's letters led to lots of talk about America. The colonists seemed to be experiencing growing frustration and dissatisfaction over a number of the acts passed by Parliament in London to regulate affairs in the American colonies. In one of his letters, Whitefield had told about a massacre that had occurred in Boston in the colony of Massachusetts on March 5, 1770. The event was known as the "Incident on King Street." William's imagination had run wild picturing the scene as he heard the details read aloud. A mob had formed around a small group of British soldiers stationed in Boston to protect the colonial officials trying to enforce the unpopular parliamentary acts. The mob shouted at the soldiers, who became fearful and, without orders to do so, began firing their rifles into the crowd. They killed five people and wounded others. Inflamed by the incident, the unrest toward Britain among the American colonists continued to grow. Uncle William, like many influential men in London, waited to see how Lord North, the new British prime minister, would deal with the American situation.

John Thornton told William of another man who fired William's imagination. The Thorntons were avid sponsors of Christian activities. Two years before, a Native American named Samson Occom had come from Connecticut to England on a preaching tour to raise money for an Indian school back in the colony. John Thornton arranged many of Occom's speaking engagements, which drew huge crowds. As he thought about what a real American Indian might be like, William wished he had been able to see and hear Samson Occom.

John Newton often came to London to visit and preach in the parlor at the house in St. James's Place. When he knew that the Reverend Newton would be in the city, William begged his uncle and aunt to let him come home for the weekend to hear the curate preach.

In August 1771, William turned twelve years old. By now he'd been living with Aunt Hannah and Uncle William for two years. In that time he'd grown to love them and felt like their son. Because they felt the same way, they made William heir to their fortune and mapped out his future, which included taking over the family business. There was just one problem. As William became more comfortable with his new Christian beliefs, his thoughts about serving God began to creep into his letters home.

Aunt Hannah warned William to be careful about what he wrote to his mother, since she believed that Methodists were fanatics. But William found it hard to believe that his own mother would judge him so harshly—that is, until there was a knock at the door one day, just before William was ready to return to school. His mother brushed the butler aside and sailed into the parlor, where she grabbed William's hand and pulled him to her. "This boy is coming home with me, now!" she announced.

"But . . ." Aunt Hannah replied.

"But what?" William's mother asked, cutting off his aunt. "It has come to my attention, in part because of William's letters home, that he has been infected with the Methodist model of religion while in your home. Is that correct?"

Uncle William stepped forward. "Elizabeth," he said, "I think we need to quiet down and speak of this together. It is indeed true that we follow certain Methodist ways and attend prayer meetings, but we have taken the lad to Church of England services every Sunday since he's been with us these two years."

"Ha!" William's mother spat. "I have spoken to his grandfather, your very father, William, about this, and he is disgusted that you would expose my son—the heir of our family—to such unattractive enthusiasms. In fact, he has told me that if William were to persist in this wretched way you have exposed him to, he would be disinherited. To quote his words, 'If

William turns Methodist, he shall not have a sixpence of mine.'"

As William stood beside his mother, he noticed his hands were shaking. Would she really take him away from Uncle William and Aunt Hannah and all the wonderful people he knew?

"Tell your manservant to pack William's things immediately. I do not want my son breathing this poisonous air one moment more than he has to."

Aunt Hannah began to cry. William's mother glared at her. "You should not fear," she said sarcastically. "If this is a work of grace, you know it cannot fail."

Uncle William walked over and put his arm around William. "Elizabeth, the boy has lost so much. I beg you to leave him here with us. He is happy and thriving. What more could you ask?"

William's mother snorted. "What more? How dare you say such a thing! I allowed him to come to you when I was very ill, and you have abused my trust—and his grandfather's. He must come home at once."

William felt his shoulders slump. His mother's voice had a tone that was not to be crossed. He knew he was going back to Hull, away from the kind and interesting people he now called friends and, worse, his fellow Methodists.

The ride home passed mainly in silence. Every so often William's mother would tell him about someone or of something interesting that had happened in Hull. His baby sister Anne was now three years old and chattering with her nursemaid. The Sykeses, a family the Wilberforces were close to, were excited that William was coming back to Hull, and they couldn't wait to invite him to stay in their country home. William knew that his mother was trying to cheer him up, but the trip home was gloomy. The only thing that brightened William was the thought of going back to Hull Grammar School with Joseph Milner as his teacher, but even that idea was squashed.

"Your grandfather says he needs to take a firm hand in your education now, or all will be lost. Unfortunately, Joseph Milner seems to have been infected with Methodist ideas himself. Every Sunday afternoon he preaches at Holy Trinity, and much of what he says contradicts the Reverend Robinson's morning sermons. Everything is being turned upside down, and your grandfather will not allow you to be taught by such a man."

William was too stunned to reply.

His mother went on. "You are forbidden to have anything to do with him. Instead, your grandfather is looking into other schools. Dr. Kingsman Baskett, the schoolmaster at Pocklington, is coming down to interview you. It will be a mercy if you get a place there—it's where your grandfather went to school—and we have been assured that Dr. Baskett is as far from sympathizing with Methodists as he is from traveling to the moon."

Chapter 3

Pulled Apart

William peered out the carriage window as Pocklington School came into view. It was a large, three-story stone building covered with ivy and surrounded by trees and green fields.

"There it is, lad," William's grandfather said. "*Virtute et Veritate.* That's what you'll learn here, to act with courage and truth. It's the school motto, you know."

"Yes, Grandfather," William said. He did not care about the school's motto or that Pocklington was over 250 years old. All he cared about was that it was not his old school in Putney and that he was not returning to live with his aunt and uncle.

William tried not to think about his life in London, but it was difficult not to. He'd come to love Aunt Hannah as much as his mother, and he certainly felt more comfortable talking things over with her. She listened to him in a way his mother never had. Being torn away from his aunt and uncle had nearly broken his heart. The only consolation was his new attachment to his three-year-old sister, Anne, who had questions about everything. Anne trailed William everywhere he went, asking questions and making comments. William loved her cheerful nature, and now, he thought gloomily, he had been taken away from her and placed in this ancient building with boys who were not rich enough or talented enough to find a school in London.

"Come on, lad, we don't have all day." The banging of his grandfather's cane on the coach floor broke into William's thoughts. "Hasn't changed much. You could do a lot worse than coming here," his grandfather commented.

William wasn't so sure as he climbed down from the coach and followed his grandfather toward the ivy-covered building and on inside. Dr. Baskett awaited them in the hallway. William listened as Dr. Baskett and his grandfather discussed his future. He was astonished when Grandfather Wilberforce offered to pay the large sum of four hundred pounds so that William could board with the Baskett family rather than stay in the dormitory with the other twenty-eight boys.

"I think William will fit in," Dr. Baskett said. "I have three boys of my own. My oldest, Kingsman, is just about the same age, and they should all get along well. They know something of hardship too."

William knew that Dr. Baskett was referring to the fact that the boys' mother, his first wife, had died two years before. He hoped that he and the Baskett boys would all be friends.

As the coach pulled up to the schoolmaster's house, which stood on the school grounds, William was glad he was not headed to the dormitory. He offered a silent prayer of thanks as the coachman placed his trunk beside his bed. Now, at least, he could read his Bible and pray in private, away from the prying eyes of the other boys.

Despite his grandfather's efforts to ease the way, it took William a long time to settle into life at Pocklington. He found he had little in common with the other students. William wrote to Aunt Hannah and Uncle William every Sunday. At first even writing their names brought tears to his eyes. He missed them deeply. His letters told of how he was determined to maintain his faith. Three months after leaving London, William wrote to Uncle William.

> My dear uncle, How good God is to me, what reason have I to be thankful; it is impossible to sum up all his mercies, and his benefits are innumerable. I will give anything I own in the world to be with you again yet I trust that everything is ordered for the best and if we put our whole trust and confidence in him we shall never be confounded.

Nine months later, just after a visit home for his thirteenth birthday, William wrote to Aunt Hannah.

> One of the greatest misfortunes I had whilst at Hull was not being able to hear the blessed

> word of God, as my mama would not let me go to high church on a Sunday afternoon; but the Lord was everyday granting me some petition, and I trust I can say that I increased in the knowledge of God and Jesus Christ whom he had sent, whom to know is life eternal.

Over time William adjusted to life at Pocklington. He found the schoolwork easy, and he had plenty of time to read poetry. On his early morning walks, he challenged himself to learn a new poem by the Scottish poet James Beattie. The poem, entitled "The Minstrel," was 558 lines long. William mastered it quickly and was often called upon to entertain his classmates by reciting it. He returned home to Hull frequently for visits, where his mother quizzed him on his religious activities. Not wanting to encourage William's Christian beliefs, she could barely tolerate his attending church with her on Sunday. Instead, she insisted William involve himself in the rounds of social events Hull was famous for. So when he was home, William found himself caught up in a whirlwind of social activity, attending the theater at Finkle Street, playing endless games of cards, and going to the assembly rooms in Digger Lane, dinner parties, and poetry readings. Being the grandson and namesake of one of Hull's most prominent citizens opened many doors for William, and his natural high spirits and showmanship kept the invitations flowing.

William felt as if he was caught between two worlds—and was being pulled apart. He wanted desperately to continue his life as a Methodist, but he was only a boy, and his mother and grandfather insisted that he take part in many things that he felt went against his faith. As a result, ever so slowly, the world of dancing, music, and card playing began to win out, until William put away his Bible and stopped writing to his aunt and uncle. It had proved too difficult for him to go on alone in his faith.

When William was home in Hull on visits, his grandfather expected him to take an interest in Wilberforce and Smith, the family mercantile business. But William found it hard to concentrate on ledgers, bills of lading, contracts of affreightment, and dunnage costs. He could not imagine being involved with such things for the rest of his life. Thankfully, it looked as if he would not have to. Uncle Abel and Aunt Mary Smith's son Abel, who was ten years older than William, loved the importing business and spent much of his time in Hull working alongside Thomas Thompson managing the booming Wilberforce and Smith Company.

The future looked bright for another reason. Uncle Abel Smith had just been elected to the House of Commons as a member for Aldborough in West Yorkshire. He'd had to pay out quite a lot of money to secure the votes needed to get himself elected, but he told William it was a shrewd business move, especially because members of Parliament received free postage. Postage rates were expensive at the time, and as Uncle Abel explained, "I will save a very considerable expense in so extensive a business as that I am engaged in."

In late November 1774, William's grandfather died at the age of eighty-four. William attended his funeral in Beverly, where his grandfather was buried in the family plot beside William's father. Six years had passed since Robert Wilberforce's funeral. William had been a boy of nine then. Now he was a young man of fifteen. As he watched his grandfather's coffin being lowered into the grave, he thought about how his grandfather had told his mother he would not inherit sixpence from him if he (William) continued in his Methodist ways. But William already knew that his grandfather had left him far more than sixpence. He was to receive many shares in the family business, along with Markington Hall, a Tudor manor house located near Harrogate. The place had belonged to William's grandmother's family, and the house and farmland around it had tenants, providing a steady income from the property.

The inheritance, most of which would be watched over for William until he turned twenty-one years of age, was a sign that William had indeed left his Methodist habits behind. They had been swallowed up in the daily life at Pocklington and his busy social calendar in Hull. Because William had received little encouragement to think about God, his views had changed a lot over the years. He'd exchanged his Christian faith for the belief that many things happen to people—good and bad—and all a person could be expected to do was endure the bad and make the most of the good. God—if He existed—was distant and remote, and human beings had to do their best to muddle through life.

Not long after his grandfather's death, William expressed these views in a class essay he wrote on patience.

> We must learn to bear whatever befalls us, so as on the one hand, not to be too much elevated or overjoyed by the smiles of prosperity, nor on the other too much depressed or cast down by the frowns of adversity. The stings of fortune, how severe soever they may seem to us, it is most likely we deserve, for we ought to learn to bear with patience what we cannot possibly avoid. Life is a very uncertain thing at best; therefore we ought not to rely upon any good fortune, since perhaps this moment we may enjoy the greatest worldly happiness, the next be plunged into the deepest abyss of unutterable misery.

William felt his own "unutterable misery" when in 1776 he learned that his younger sister, Anne, had died of fever. Anne was eight years old, a vivacious girl who made William laugh. William found it difficult to believe that she was gone. It brought back memories of her birth, just before their father had died. William also thought of his father, who would have understood what William was feeling at that moment. Robert Wilberforce was one of eleven children, only four of whom survived to adulthood.

Now it was just William and his sister Sally, whom he rarely saw, since she was far away at boarding school. Anne's death reminded William of how lonely and depressing life could be. At seventeen years of age he felt he'd lost so many of the people he loved, either through death or through forced separation.

By now William was coming to the end of his days at Pocklington School, and he was unsure what to do next. He received an allowance from his grandfather's inheritance until he was old enough to control all the money and property left him. Even with the security of that money, he had to decide on his next step in life. No one in his family had gone on to university, but Dr. Baskett insisted that William would do well at St. John's College, Cambridge. "I went there myself, as you well know," he told William, "and I think you would enjoy the social scene. You love poetry. You could study that and continue with your Latin and Greek."

William considered attending St. John's. He liked the idea of spending three or more years at university before he had to make a decision about what to do with his life. Not that that was such a pressing issue. With his cousin Abel Smith running the family business so well, combined with the inheritance from his grandfather, William would have enough money to live on for a long time to come.

In October 1776, William enrolled in St. John's College, Cambridge. His first night at the college opened his eyes to what lay ahead for a rich, young student such as he.

Chapter 4

He Had Found His Calling

"Look around you, Wilberforce," William Arnald, St. John's College's head tutor and fellow, said as he slapped William on the back. "A young man like you . . . How old are you?"

"Seventeen," William replied. "I just turned seventeen years old."

"Old enough. Old enough. I'm here to tell you that there are three kinds of young men at Cambridge, as you'll soon find out. There are those who are destined to work in the church. You don't want to overinvolve yourself with them. They study and pray the day away. Then there are the ambitious young men who want to be lawyers. You'll see them sitting in the difficult classes, laboring over dusty law books in the library and perfecting their Latin. And then there's the third group—the young men who will be somebody in the world by virtue of their family name and wealth."

William watched as the head tutor raised his tankard and took a large gulp of ale before going on. "Young men like you, Wilberforce, don't need to study at Cambridge. You don't need honors. You already have everything you need. Instead, young men like you should enjoy themselves, broaden their outlook on life, make friends, host parties. When you leave here, your friends will prove far more valuable than any degree."

As he took a sip of his own ale, William looked around. He and the head tutor were sitting in the college dining hall with its high Gothic arches and polished wooden tables. It was proving hard for William to take in what he was hearing. Dr. Baskett at Pocklington had always urged him to study harder, think of his future, and learn all he could. Now, at Cambridge, one of the best universities in England, William was being encouraged by his tutor not to take his studies too seriously.

In a way the tutor's words made perfect sense. William's inheritance had made him wealthy, and while he had access only to an allowance from it at present, it was a generous one. William wondered if perhaps he should spend some of it on making friends and having fun.

"Ah," William Arnald said, turning and looking over his shoulder. "Here come a couple of young men from Ireland who know how to enjoy themselves. James, Daniel, come over here and meet William Wilberforce. I have no doubt he can play a good hand of cards." He turned back to William. "You can play, can't you?"

"Of course," William laughed. "I cut my teeth on the ace of spades."

"Well, then," James said, shaking William's hand. "How about you join us in my room after dinner and we'll see what you're made of."

That night William joined his two new friends as they played cards and drank until the early hours of the morning.

William woke the next day with a headache and determined he wouldn't be attending lectures that day—or any other day for that matter. His new friends had told him that attending lectures was not compulsory and only the bookish students bothered to go to them. That suited William fine, and within a week or two, his room was a hive of activity day and night. He loved entertaining his new friends and ordered a constant supply of Yorkshire pies from a local baker, each pie weighing about thirty pounds. Fellow students dropped by at any time for a meal of cold pie and ale, along with a good story or two, and, if they were fortunate, an impromptu concert from William. He loved to sing and invited his friends who played string instruments to accompany him.

Life soon settled into an easy routine for William. Sometimes he studied classical literature, but he stayed away from mathematics. If his tutor caught him studying, he would laugh and remind William that he was not at Cambridge to embark upon a career.

William played hundreds of games of cards with James Hardy, Daniel Sullivan, and their friends. He lost a little money now and then in these games, but the thrill of winning was worth it. William also had some studious acquaintances, like the student in the room behind his. Thomas Gisborne was studying to become an Anglican minister and took his studies seriously, but even he could be lured into William's room late in the evening. William would pick up the fire tongs and rap them on the back of his fireplace. He knew that Thomas would hear the din and come over for a glass of sherry and a slice of Yorkshire pie. Sometimes the two young men would talk and joke until the small hours of the morning. And although Thomas had to think about going to lectures later in the morning, William could sleep in until lunchtime if he wanted.

Because William was a quick learner, he managed to scrape through his examinations. William Arnald encouraged him. "Thomas Gisborne is very clever, but then he studies all the time. You, on the other hand, are clever enough to get by with hardly studying at all." The tutor's words were music to William's ears.

During the holidays William sometimes went home to Hull, but he often preferred to accompany his new friends to their homes. One of his favorite places was the Lake District of northwest England, with its lakes, forests, and mountains. Two of William's friends, William Cookson and Edward Christian, both lived in the Lake District, and William would often accompany them home. He also made friends with Gerard Edwards, another wealthy student whose family had made their fortune draining the fens in the east of England. William also liked to go home with Gerard.

During his second Christmas at Cambridge, in 1777, William learned that Uncle William Wilberforce, whom he'd lived with in London, had died at the age of fifty-six. For a moment William felt a wince of regret. His uncle and aunt had been so kind to him and such earnest Christians. Now, at eighteen years of age, William found his present life to be so different from the one they had encouraged him to lead. William was not surprised to learn that his uncle, who was childless, had left him most of his wealth, along with Lauriston House in Wimbledon, with its three acres of manicured lawns and gardens.

Following Christmas and New Year 1778, William returned to Cambridge for the spring term. This time he decided to make some changes. He would study a little more and keep away from all-night card games. This was difficult for him at first, but as William focused more on his studies, it became clear to him that he didn't have a plan for his life after Cambridge. With his uncle's estate added to his inheritance from his grandfather, William knew he would not have to earn a penny for the rest of his life. But that did not mean he couldn't do something. The question was, what?

The things that he enjoyed most were singing, debating, and meeting new people, but none of those seemed like serious pursuits—that is, until October 1778, when William's cousin Abel Smith entered politics, following in his father's footsteps. William's cousin used the Smith family money and their banking influence to smooth the way to becoming the member of Parliament for the city of Nottingham, his hometown. Abel served in Parliament for only three months before he fell ill and died suddenly on January 22, 1779. William was sad for his aunt and uncle as he remembered the death of their oldest son, Thomas, ten years before. William's cousin Robert, Uncle Abel and Aunt Mary's third son, took over Abel's seat in Parliament, and William decided to go to see Robert speak in the House of Commons.

William traveled to London and stayed in Lauriston House at Wimbledon. One of the required terms of his uncle's will in inheriting the place was that Aunt Hannah be allowed to live in the house for the rest of her life. Hannah, however, had vacated the property, preferring to live right in London. Lauriston House was now William's to use as he wished, and it was just seven miles from Westminster Palace, where Parliament was held.

Westminster Palace was located beside the Thames. It had once been a royal palace before becoming the seat of Parliament, where both the House of Commons and the House of Lords met. William made his way to St. Stephen's Chapel, the old royal chapel where the House of Commons now met. He entered the Stranger's Gallery, located along both sides of the building above the wood-paneled chamber below. As he looked for a seat in the gallery, a young man beckoned him. William made his way over, and the young man introduced himself as William Pitt, a student at Pembroke College, Cambridge. William vaguely recognized William Pitt from Cambridge, if by no other way than his height. William

Pitt was six feet tall, while William was only five foot two. Since the two attended different colleges, they had little to do with each other.

William soon discovered that William Pitt was a serious student who had started at Pembroke at age fourteen. Even though he and William were the same age, William Pitt was three years ahead in his studies. He had already earned a bachelor's degree and was now working on a law degree. Seated side by side, the two Williams peered down at the proceedings on the floor of the House of Commons. William wished he knew more about who the people down there were and what they were talking about.

As he watched the proceedings, William became aware that William Pitt was totally familiar with all that was going on. And so he should be. He explained that he came from a long line of English politicians. His great-grandfather, Thomas Pitt, had been the governor of Madras, India, before returning to England to become a member of Parliament (MP). His grandfather, Robert Pitt, had also been an MP, as had his father, William Pitt the elder, also known as the Earl of Chatham. William Pitt the elder had served as prime minister of Great Britain in the 1760s. William remembered the elder Pitt's death just a year before and how the people of Great Britain had mourned him as their champion. William realized that if he wanted to know what was going on in Parliament, William Pitt was the person to ask. Pitt had been groomed for a life in politics since he was a boy.

Following their meeting, the two Williams spent many hours together talking about politics, and they had a lot to discuss. William Pitt explained to William how the two chambers of Parliament worked. Members of the House of Commons were elected by voters to represent local constituencies. Each county in the country elected two representatives to the House of Commons. Within these counties were a number of boroughs, which also elected two representatives to the Commons. Many of these boroughs had been established centuries before, and over time, as the population shifted, they had become very small. Pitt explained that the borough of Old Sarum now had only seven voters living in it who could elect two members to Parliament, and the borough of Dunwich, which had almost completely disappeared into the sea because of erosion, could also elect two members.

Wealthy lords and landowners controlled many of the boroughs and influenced who got elected to Parliament in them. In some boroughs almost all the residents rented from the lord, and if they failed to vote for the candidate the lord wanted elected, they were in danger of being evicted from their homes. A candidate elected to the House of Commons from these constituencies was considered to be in the pocket of the lord. Hence, these constituencies were referred to as "pocket boroughs." In other small boroughs a candidate could get himself elected simply by paying eligible voters to vote for him. These boroughs were referred to as "rotten boroughs." William was surprised by the blatant corruption involved in getting elected, but William Pitt assured him it was all considered a normal part of politics in England.

While it was the job of the House of Commons to make laws by passing bills, those bills were then reviewed by the House of Lords, to which the lords were appointed for life by the king. As the lords reviewed the bills, the House of Lords could then amend or veto them, forcing the House of Commons to reconsider and change a bill to the liking of the lords. The House of Lords could also propose legislation, but only the House of Commons could initiate bills that levied taxes. The ability of the lords to manipulate voting to get their candidates elected to the House of Commons and the lords' power to veto bills meant that the House of Lords wielded a great deal of power, which often led to infighting between the two chambers.

William Pitt also explained that like his father, he was opposed to the British fighting the American colonists. He thought that Great Britain, and particularly King George III, was being unrealistic, that the country could never win a war against a land as vast as North America. It seemed to William Pitt that the government wasn't quite sure whether it should wage a ruthless and destructive war or try to induce the misguided subjects in the American colonies to return to the care of their mother country. William Pitt's father's idea had been to make peace with the American colonists, but the king and Lord North, the British prime minister, would have none of it. King George seemed determined to hold onto the American colonies at all costs. However, the cost of the war in the colonies was taking its toll on the British economy. Parliament called for economic reform in the country, but Lord North was opposed to this.

The situation led to many lively debates in the House of Commons, and over the winter of 1779–1780, William Wilberforce and William Pitt spent hours in the Stranger's Gallery watching the debates. The main players in them were all excellent orators. William watched enthralled as Lord North defended the government's position from attacks by Charles Fox, Edmund Burke, and others opposed to the war. William was fascinated by the way they used a mixture of voice control, witty phrases, and literary and historical references to make their points.

The more William watched these great politicians in action, the more he knew that this was the life for him. He had found his calling: he wanted to be a politician debating among the most elite group of people in the land. Of course, William was not yet sure of his political convictions and what exactly he would debate about in the House of Commons. But as he and William Pitt argued and debated long into the nights, William found himself persuaded to agree with William Pitt on just about every important point.

The two Williams decided to enter politics together. They would make a tight team. William Wilberforce was outgoing, witty, and new to politics, while William Pitt was brilliant and shy, with politics running through his veins. They faced just one issue: they were both born in 1759—William Pitt in May and William Wilberforce in August. But English law decreed that a candidate must be twenty-one years old to be voted into Parliament. Normally this would not have been a problem. The two Williams would have waited until they were both twenty-one and then for an election to be called. But elections were not held at regular intervals. Rather, they occurred when Parliament got bogged down and seemed to be achieving very little. Then the prime minister would petition the king to dissolve Parliament and call for an election. A prime minister, of course, would ask the king for a parliamentary election at a time advantageous to his administration. Further, a prime minister in favor with the king had substantial behind-the-scenes influence over an election's outcome. Therefore, new elections would bring a new Parliament, but not typically a new government. A government—the prime minister and his administration, or cabinet—remained in power until forced out by the king or Parliament.

Both young men wanted to be in the House of Commons when a new Parliament was seated. William Pitt told William that that was the time when they would have the best chance of bringing about some real change in the country and ending the war in the colonies. The unpredictability of Lord North's timetable presented a challenge to the two Williams, who realized that the timing of a new election was everything. It was no use running for a seat if they were still too young to take it up. Given the raucous debate over the war in the American colonies, as well as the deteriorating British economy, most people expected that a new election would be called any day, or at least before the end of 1780. If that happened and the two Williams were not yet twenty-one, they could not be official candidates, and any campaigning they may have done would be for nothing. Nevertheless, as the two men talked about it, they decided to take a gamble and start canvassing for the future election. William Pitt declared that he would run for the seat in Cambridge, while William

Wilberforce declared for Hull. It made sense for William to run for a seat in Parliament from Hull. His family was well-known and liked there. In fact, the family had just given a large sum of money to help build a new dock in the town, something that could only help William get elected.

William faced obstacles, however. Hull, like all the other boroughs in England, sent two men as representatives to Parliament. In 1780 these two men were Lord Robert Manners and David Hartley. As William sized up the situation, he realized that Lord Robert would be tough to beat. He had been in Parliament for thirty-three years and was the uncle of the Duke of Rutland, an important man in the area. Moreover, the government directed their men as to whom to vote for, and they backed Lord Robert. Since a garrison of soldiers was now based in Hull, Lord Robert was assured of their vote and thus one of the seats in Parliament.

Hull's other seat was held by David Hartley, an eccentric inventor who enjoyed the backing of the great Yorkshire houses of the Marquess of Rockingham and Sir George Savile. As he sized up the situation, William decided that he had a better chance of beating David Hartley in the election, despite Hartley's powerful backing. While Hartley was the son of a prominent philosopher, he held some strange views. He corresponded with Benjamin Franklin in the Pennsylvania colony, and he strongly believed that the king should grant all the American colonies their independence. This was a point William thought he could highlight to his advantage.

Although William understood and even sympathized with Hartley's views, he knew that many of the voters in Hull feared that letting the American colonies go would affect the money they made from trade. William knew that he could stir up that fear and win some votes for himself. Politics seemed to William like a giant game of chess: the man who manipulates the pieces the best and outmaneuvers his opponent wins.

William had another way to outmaneuver David Hartley: he could buy votes. This was a common practice throughout England, with voters expecting a payment of two pounds and two shillings from a candidate for their vote. Of course this would take some money, since Hull, with a population of fifteen thousand, had eleven hundred men who were eligible to vote.

In May 1780, William returned to Hull to begin his political campaign. It was a mixed success. Johnny Bell, a local butcher, became such a zealous supporter that he offered to kill a man who had thrown a rock at William during a campaign speech. William quickly talked him out of murder and into giving the man "a good fright."

Many people liked William but were committed to vote for the other two candidates. Nonetheless, William kept on campaigning. He also made frequent visits to London and Cambridge, where he compared notes with William Pitt. It seemed that try as he may, William Pitt was struggling to get votes in the Cambridge electorate. William encouraged him as best he could, but he had his own votes to think about.

So when he was in London, he would visit the taverns in Wapping, beside the docks. Many merchants from Hull lived in the area, and William worked hard to persuade them to return to Hull and cast their votes for him when an election was called. He also offered them the going rate of ten pounds each to pay their expenses for their trip. William had no qualms about doing this. He knew that other candidates did much worse. Some of them even "cooped" men who would vote against them. Cooping involved kidnapping potential voters and locking them inside taverns until the election was over. By the time the men were released, they were so drunk they didn't even know where they had been or what had happened to them.

All the while William hunted down any available information on how Parliament was doing. He knew that Lord North could call for a new election at any moment. It was a race against time. He just hoped this would occur after his birthday.

When August 24, 1780, arrived and Lord North had not called for the dissolution of Parliament and a new election, William breathed a sigh of relief. He looked forward to the huge birthday party he had planned for everyone in Hull that night. He had already spent eight thousand pounds on his bid to get elected to Parliament, and he would spend another five hundred pounds on a spectacular twenty-first birthday party for himself.

William invited everyone he knew and many others he did not know to a huge ox-roast and bonfire. A day and a half before, an ox weighing eight hundred pounds was dressed whole by William's new friend and supporter, the butcher Johnny Bell, and placed on a spit over the bonfire. It took nearly thirty hours for the meat to cook all the way through.

By Thursday night, not only was the ox cooked, but also several fields outside town had been transformed into an outdoor party venue. It was a beautiful summer night, and people flowed in for the party. Hogsheads of ale also flowed freely in the moonlight. It was one of the happiest days William could remember. His mother and sister were there, along with many old neighbors and friends from Hull, and, of course, many voters.

The following morning news arrived from London that on August 24 Lord North had advised the king to dissolve Parliament and call for a new election. William Wilberforce had turned twenty-one years old that very day and was now eligible to be elected to Parliament. He took it as a good omen.

Chapter 5

The Youngest Member of Parliament

Eighteen days after his twenty-first birthday, William waited anxiously outside the Guildhall in Hull for the results of the election. He was astonished when they were made public. He had won by a landslide, receiving half the votes. Lord Robert came in second and David Hartley, third. Lord Robert and William would be the two MPs representing Hull. Not only that, William would be the youngest member of Parliament.

Just as astonishing to William was the fact that his friend William Pitt would not be joining him in Parliament. Pitt had lost his bid for election, coming in last in the voting at Cambridge. Instead he took the bar exams to become a lawyer and promised William he would find a way to join him in Westminster as soon as possible.

On October 31, 1780, William Wilberforce took his seat in the House of Commons. As he sat on the members' bench, he looked up at the Stranger's Gallery and thought of the hours he had sat up there looking down and observing all that was happening on the floor of the House. And now here he was, a member of Parliament. It was hard to believe. He had just graduated from Cambridge and was now one of 558 representatives elected to help govern the country.

In the House of Commons, the two elected members from each county and borough, along with the lords, tried to exert pressure on other members to form political alliances, back particular bills, and vote in certain ways on various issues. William entered Parliament determined to stay clear of such alliances and remain independent, voting as he saw fit on various issues and bills.

Business in the House of Commons began immediately. There was the usual round of discussions and votes on taxes, importing and exporting, and road building and maintenance. The successful completion of the first iron bridge in England, over the Severn River, was noted in the House, as was news of Captain James Cook being speared to death by natives in the Sandwich Islands in the South Pacific.

Parliament also debated the volatile topic of the American colonies and the shifting world order that had resulted from the war there with the colonists for their independence. Members of Parliament were particularly concerned about the American navy patrolling the Atlantic Ocean and harassing British trade in the Caribbean by stopping ships from reaching British ports there. These actions were also putting trade from India at risk.

Through the fighting in America, the British had also been drawn into war with France and Spain, and French warships now harassed British ships. It seemed to William that Great Britain was at war with half the world, while Prussia, Russia, and the Scandinavian countries had banded together to declare their right to remain neutral in the ongoing military struggle, leaving the British with few allies. There was also unrest in Ireland, and across the English Channel, French peasants were stirring up trouble in their country.

Upon arrival in the House of Commons, William decided it would be best to keep his eyes open and mouth shut. He watched as other members rose to make their speeches and arguments. He noted how others reacted: which members respected each other, who could listen to an argument and change his mind, and who was already closed to new ideas and ways of dealing with the issues Great Britain faced. Although William was determined to remain independent, he found himself in agreement with most of the policies put forward by the Earl of Shelburne and the Marquess of Rockingham.

Now that he would be working in London, William rented rooms within easy walking distance of Westminster Palace and set out to make as many friends as he could. This was not a difficult task for him. London had several men's clubs where the important people in the city gathered. William joined five of these clubs: White's, Brooks's, Boodle's, Miles's, and Evans's. Each club offered dinner in the evening, along with high-stakes gambling and endless drinking. The clubs suited William well, and he soon had all the friends he could wish for. On those evenings when he was not frequenting one or another of the clubs, he could be found at the opera or theater. On the weekends he invited fellow members of Parliament and various club members back to Lauriston House at Wimbledon. William Pitt often spent time there too, scheming of ways to get into Parliament.

In January 1781, following the Christmas recess, William was pleased to learn that William Pitt would be joining him in Parliament. Sir James Lowther, at the request of the Duke of Rutland, had bought him a seat in a by-election, a special election held to fill a vacancy when someone dies or resigns from office. William Pitt was welcomed to Parliament as a member for Appleby, a rotten borough in Westmorland.

It wasn't long before the two Williams were seated side by side in the House of Commons, and the men dined together almost every night. They strategized about how to govern Great Britain. Parliament was still dominated by the war with the American colonies and the opportunities it gave for other European nations to poke at England's defenses. But in February 1781 some good news arrived. The British had captured and taken control of the Dutch Caribbean island of Sint Eustatius, which had supplied the rebellious colonists in North America with most of their weapons. More victories followed. In March the British beat Major General Nathanael Greene and his men at the Battle of Guilford Courthouse in North Carolina, and in July, Lord Cornwallis defeated French forces led by the Marquis de Lafayette at the Battle of Green Spring in Virginia.

By the time Parliament's summer recess rolled around, William's mind was awhirl with all manner of things affecting Great Britain. He decided to retreat to the country for the recess. He rented a cottage named Rayrigg on the banks of Lake Windermere in the Lake District and packed a huge pile of books to take with him. William intended to read the classics, as well as history, legal statutes, and poetry.

Rayrigg turned out to be a beautiful, quiet cottage—that is, until all the visitors descended on William. His mother and sister came to stay, as did many fellow members of Parliament. Instead of quiet reading, William's summer was filled with punting on the lake, horseback riding, and parties.

By the time summer recess was over, the tide had turned in favor of the Americans in the war. In late August, the French fleet under the command of Comte de Grasse sailed into Chesapeake Bay, blocking Lord Cornwallis and his troops from escaping by sea, and a siege had begun in Yorktown.

During the winter session of Parliament, William continued to observe and say little. He did make two short speeches on issues affecting his constituents in Hull: one was on a bill to prevent smuggling, and the other involved shipping taxes.

William Pitt, on the other hand, was an excellent speaker in the House of Commons. His political knowledge was vast, and there didn't seem to be an issue that came before the House whose various nuances he was not aware of. On one occasion, without time to prepare, he was asked to make a speech in support of economic reforms called for by Edmund Burke.

William watched as his friend stood and began to speak. William could hardly believe what he was hearing. Pitt's speech was masterful. Afterward William wrote to a friend in Hull, declaring, "The papers will have informed you how Mr. William Pitt, second son of the late Lord Chatham, has distinguished himself; he comes out as his father did a ready-made orator, and I doubt not but that I shall one day or other see him the first man in the country. His famous speech, however, did not convince me, and I [voted] with [Lord North], the old fat fellow."

During this time, the two Williams helped establish their own men's club at Goostree's, located at 51 Pall Mall. The club had only about twenty-five members, all young MPs who were graduates of Cambridge. Most were independent members, and William Pitt was their natural leader.

William was relieved that no one at Goostree's gambled large sums of money. He had already stopped gambling at the other fashionable clubs, not because he lost money, but because he won too much. One evening at Brooks's Club, he had been delighted at first to win six hundred pounds, but as he listened to the whispers of the men he'd won it from, he realized they did not have the money to pay and would need to get loans from family members to settle their gambling debt. This shocked William.

It was easy for him to forget that not all his friends had access to the kind of money he did. Either they had not inherited their fortunes yet, or they were younger brothers, like William Pitt, who received only a small amount of money, with the bulk of the family's land and other assets going to the oldest brother. Once William realized his winning was causing someone else hardship, he quit gambling. It wasn't fun anymore.

As William's reputation as a gambler fell, his reputation as a singer rose. He was even asked to sing at the Duchess of Devonshire's ball, where the Prince of Wales declared that he would go anywhere to hear William sing.

Every night at Goostree's the Cambridge men would sit and drink and talk, William Pitt's bottle of port wine always close at hand. Pitt had told William when they first met that the doctor had diagnosed him with gout at the age of fourteen and prescribed that he drink a bottle of port wine a day for the rest of his life as a treatment for the condition. As the men talked, the discussion would usually turn to the progress of the war in America and how it was affecting life in England. Everyone agreed that from the beginning, Lord North, as prime minister, had mishandled the situation in the American colonies. Then, in late 1781, word reached England of the surrender of Lord Cornwallis and his British troops to General George Washington at Yorktown, Virginia, on October 19. Lord North, however, refused to concede that the American Revolutionary War was over and that Great Britain had lost.

Following the Christmas recess, things came to a head. The men at Goostree's no longer believed that Lord North could lead the country. He still refused to admit the war was over, and his refusal to consider other options to end the standoff in North America in the first place had not only cost Britain her most prized colonies but also caused war with other European countries and turmoil inside England itself. It was time for Lord North to step down as prime minister.

On February 22, 1782, William Wilberforce gave his first speech in Parliament on an issue other than those affecting his electorate in Hull. He launched into a stirring speech calling for the government to accept the end of the war in the colonies, declaring that the way in which Lord North and his ministers had conducted themselves toward the war "resembled the career of furious madmen rather than the prudent exertions of statesmen." He also lambasted them for pursuing the ruinous war in a "cruel, bloody, impractical manner."

Several days later William Pitt gave a stirring speech, challenging Lord North to accept the end of the war. "What I have now offered is meant merely for the sake of my country, for the simple question is, will you change your Ministers and keep the Empire, or keep your Ministers and lose the Kingdom?" he asked.

By the end of March, Parliament's vote of no confidence against the government of Lord North led to North's resignation as prime minister.

The opposition wasted no time. The two Williams were summoned to a meeting with Charles Fox and the Earl of Shelburne. Despite the fact that Fox and Shelburne despised each other, the two men were determined to form a new government with Lord Rockingham as their leader. While it was the king's right to appoint the prime minister, these days a British monarch had a chance to govern effectively only if his prime minister had sufficient support in Parliament. This meant that the king had to negotiate with influential lords and MPs such as Shelburne and Fox, particularly if he wanted able politicians to serve in the new government's cabinet rather than work to impede the new government and bring it down.

Being involved in the formation of a new government was a heady experience for William, who at twenty-two years of age was talking with the most powerful men in England about the future of their country. However, both Williams were cautious. It was a dangerous time to align too closely with any administration. William Pitt, who had been around politics since birth, warned William to watch and wait and, most of all, to stay well clear of accepting any minor role in a new government. "It's a way to be chopped like mincemeat," William Pitt warned. "Never accept a subordinate position."

The two of them sat together in the House of Commons as Lord Rockingham was sworn in as the new prime minister. Charles Fox and the Earl of Shelburne would serve as secretaries of state in the new government.

Lord Rockingham liked William and invited him to his home to dine. Much to William's surprise, he hinted that he might give William a peerage, making him a member of the British nobility. William's family, though extremely wealthy, were commoners. The suggestion that he, the son and grandson of merchants, would become an elite noble was astonishing and a lot for William to digest. But before Lord Rockingham could follow through on his plan to elevate William to a peerage, he caught influenza and died on July 1, 1782. He had been in office as prime minister for fourteen weeks. Once again the government of Great Britain was in turmoil, and William was glad he had taken William Pitt's advice and not become entangled in Lord Rockingham's government.

The king, who appointed the prime minister, now had a serious problem. Politically, it was obvious that he would have to replace Lord Rockingham with either Charles Fox or the Earl of Shelburne, both able and experienced politicians. But the two men disliked each other so much that if one of them was elevated to prime minister, the other would surely resign, not from his seat in Parliament, but from his position in government, refusing to serve in the other's administration. In the end King George III chose the Earl of Shelburne to be the next prime minister. And as William Pitt had predicted, Charles Fox, along with his followers and most of Lord Rockingham's supporters, resigned from their positions in government. This created an opening for William Pitt, who was made the new chancellor of the Exchequer, responsible for all economic and financial matters in the new government, as well as becoming the leader of the House of Commons.

From the beginning, Lord North and Charles Fox, themselves rivals, plotted together to bring down the Earl of Shelburne, who was not in a strong position politically. It took them only seven months to succeed. In February 1783, the Earl of Shelburne resigned as prime minister.

The collapse of the Earl of Shelburne's government led to a lot of lively conversation and speculation at Goostree's Club. The young Cambridge-educated members of Parliament tried to figure out what the king might do to solve the political crisis that had arisen. What King George III did shocked William Wilberforce and the men of Goostree's Club. He asked one of their number—William Pitt—to be the next prime minister of Great Britain. William could scarcely believe it.

Chapter 6

Crisis and Opportunity

I can't do it," William Pitt said, shaking his head at William Wilberforce. It was late February 1783, and the two Williams were spending the weekend together at Lauriston House in Wimbledon.

"You're going to turn down the king, even after you said you would accept the position of prime minister?" William asked.

"I should never have agreed," William Pitt replied. "I've had more time to think about it. I know it would never work. Lord North is too cunning to let me get anywhere. He will pretend he supports me, until the right moment, and then he will swoop in with his supporters and bring down my government. His ambition is larger than his desire to cooperate. Besides, the king hates North and Fox, and he will not tolerate North's meddling for long. I can't take the risk of going down with North."

"I believe I have to agree with you," William said. "It would be best to wait and see what happens. Pity the poor man who takes on the post. So far we've served under three prime ministers, and we've only been in the game for two years and one month. It's not a promising prospect. Better to wait until this next government falls apart and pick up the pieces."

William Pitt nodded. "As the saying goes, 'Old age and treachery will overcome youth and skill.' Lord North could be our downfall. We'll have to be on our guard if we're to come out of this with our reputations in order. I think it would be a good idea to stand together."

That's exactly what all the young MPs at Goostree's and several others, about forty in all, did. They formed themselves into a club called the Independents. Most were opposed to Lord North and Charles Fox, and they agreed together that they would not accept plum political appointments or positions that gave them a title but required little work in return for their political allegiance. They would remain independent and vote according to their conscience.

With William Pitt not willing to take the position of prime minister, King George III was forced to accept a new government formed by Lord North and Charles Fox. The two men, while rivals, agreed that although they would share power between them, a puppet prime minster needed to be put in place by the king. It was easy enough to convince the Duke of Portland to take the job. And so King George III appointed William Cavendish-Bentinck, Duke of Portland, prime minister on April 2, 1783.

Five months later, on September 3, the British government signed the Treaty of Paris. The war with the American colonies was officially over. In the treaty the British recognized their former colonies as the new country of the United States of America.

It wasn't long before William's prediction concerning the North-Fox government proved correct. He had told William Pitt, "Better to wait until this next government falls apart and pick up the pieces." When Charles Fox presented the East India Bill to Parliament, things began to fall apart. The bill involved another of Great Britain's foreign interests—India. The East India Company had received a written royal charter from Queen Elizabeth I in 1600, granting the company complete control of the vast British trade in India, including huge amounts of salt, saltpeter for gunpowder, tea, opium, silk, and indigo dye, all of which were produced in India and shipped back to England or to other British colonies. This had made the shareholders of the East India Company, including many members of Parliament, very rich.

Over the years, however, the East India Company had grown bigger and bigger, and most MPs agreed that the company needed to be reformed. Charles Fox presented to Parliament the East India Bill, which would appoint a board of seven commissioners to oversee the company. The trouble was that these seven commissioners would all be men who were supporters of Charles Fox. The two Williams were alarmed, as were a number of other members of the House of Commons. If the East India Bill passed, these new commissioners would owe Charles Fox many favors, and Fox would have a large say in what happened in India. The debate in Parliament about the bill dragged on for weeks.

In early September 1783, a week or so after the signing of the Treaty of Paris, and with debate on the East India Bill not making any progress, William Wilberforce, William Pitt, and their fellow Goostree's member Edward Eliot decided they needed a break and planned a trip to France. They left from Dover on September 12. After a rocky crossing of the English Channel, they landed in Calais, from where they made their way to Rheims. That was when all three men realized that each of them had left it to one of the others to bring a formal letter of introduction. Without the letter the men could not meet or stay with members of the French nobility. The three men paid for this huge oversight. The only person who welcomed them in Rheims was a local grocer, who let them stay with him. After the men had spent two weeks with little to do and no social engagements, the archbishop of Rheims sent a representative to see if the three Englishmen who claimed to be members of Parliament, yet knew only the local grocer, really were who they said they were.

Once the archbishop realized that they were indeed members of Parliament, he invited the two Williams and Edward Eliot to his estate, where they hunted and drank fine wine. The archbishop was also kind enough to arrange for them to be taken to Fontainebleau, seventy-five miles away, to be presented to Louis XVI and his wife, Queen Marie Antoinette.

William thought the king of France a strange man with huge boots, but he liked Queen Marie. She was young and pretty and teased all three of them about their stay with the grocer at Rheims. Once the men had met the king and queen, French society opened up to them. The men moved north to Paris, where they were soon dining with the Marquis de Lafayette, who had helped the Americans gain independence; Benjamin Franklin, who was still in Paris following the signing of the Treaty of Paris; and Franklin's fourteen-year-old grandson, Benjamin Bache.

No one was surprised when a messenger arrived on October 24 asking William Pitt to return immediately to Parliament. The East India Bill looked as though it might pass, placing enormous power in the hands of Charles Fox and his friends. William Pitt left that night for London, and William Wilberforce and Edward Eliot followed two days later.

Despite the best efforts of its opponents, in December a vote in the House of Commons passed the East India Bill, and it looked set to pass in the House of Lords as well. King George III, who despised the bill, was desperate. In a last-ditch effort to stop its passage, he sent a letter to each member of the House of Lords stating, "I would consider all who vote for it [the East India Bill] as my enemies." To make doubly sure of the bill's defeat, the next day, December 18, 1783, King George dismissed the Duke of Portland and announced that William Pitt would become the next prime minister of Great Britain.

It was a heady moment for the members of Goostree's Club. Their leader, William Pitt, at age twenty-four was the youngest ever British prime minister. And William Wilberforce was one of his most trusted allies. Others were not so pleased by the king's choice for prime minister. The *Morning Herald* published a jingle:

A sight to make surrounding nations stare
A Kingdom trusted to a schoolboy's care.

William Pitt's job soon proved impossible. The members of Parliament could not agree on anything, and no new bills were passed into law. Parliament was at a stalemate. Only one thing could change that—a new election.

To help move the cause for a new election forward, in late March 1784, William Pitt asked William Wilberforce to attend a county meeting in Yorkshire, the largest and most powerful county in England. The aim of the meeting was to encourage the county voters to urge the king to call for a new election.

On the morning of March 25, 1784, as William sat in his coach, bumping along the rutted roads on his way to the Yorkshire meeting, another plan began to form in his head. Perhaps, instead of observing the meeting and making a speech on behalf of Pitt, he could put himself forward to become one of the representatives for Yorkshire County when the new election was called. At first William wondered where the idea had come from. It was ridiculous to think that the great lords of Yorkshire—the Duke of Norfolk, Lord George Cavendish, and Lord Carlisle, all of whom would be at the meeting—would allow a young merchant from Hull to represent the whole of Yorkshire. That position had always gone to a powerful person of high birth.

The meeting was held on the huge lawn of York Castle, where four thousand voters from all over the county stood in the cold and wind. One by one the most important men in Yorkshire stood behind a table under a wooden canopy to address the crowd. The wind howled, and William stood near the front listening to every word that was said. But as the time passed, even he began to wonder if the speeches would ever end. After six hours the crowd was thoroughly wet and shivering, but each man remained standing on the lawn listening.

At four o'clock in the afternoon, after the last speaker had finished, the chairman beckoned to William. "Would you like to speak to us?" he asked.

William wondered if the crowd would stay for one more address, but this was his only chance. He leapt up onto the table the other speakers had stood behind so that he would be easily seen and heard by all. The wind picked up as William began his speech. The first thing he talked about was the East India Bill and how it would give Charles Fox and his friends tremendous power. He went on to talk about the need for a new election to break the stalemate in Parliament. The more William spoke, the more impassioned he became. The crowd stood firm, listening even as rain turned to hail.

An hour passed, and no one moved. William knew he had to finish his speech before the sun went down. As he tried to think of a suitable ending, he noticed a messenger on horseback galloping onto the castle lawn. The crowd parted as the messenger, wearing his official silver badge, made his way to the table William was standing on. William reached out and took the leather pouch from the messenger. He unbuckled the strap and pulled out a letter. It was from William Pitt, dated noon of the day before. The messenger had ridden through the night to get to York and present the letter to William.

As he scanned the letter, William realized he'd been handed the most dramatic finish to his speech. "I have in my hand," he said with a flourish, holding the letter aloft and noting that every eye was on him, "a letter from the prime minister, William Pitt. Yesterday King George III dissolved Parliament and called for a new election. The issue on which we meet has already been fixed. We are now to decide upon a solemn crisis. Each of you will now have to do what is right for our nation."

William stopped speaking. As he put the letter back in the pouch, someone in the crowd yelled, "We'll have this man for our county member!" Many other voices from the crowd joined in the call. William had won them over with his riveting performance.

Following the meeting, supporters of William Pitt, whom the newspapers were now calling "Pittites," met at York Tavern, where they shouted "Bravo, little Wilberforce" and "Wilberforce forever!" Money was pledged to run William's election campaign for the new Parliament. When he finally went to bed that night, William was well on his way to becoming a candidate to represent Yorkshire County in the upcoming election. The official title of such a representative was the Knight of the Shire for the County of Yorkshire.

The next day the local newspaper stated, "Mr. Wilberforce made a most argumentative and eloquent speech, which was listened to with the most eager attention and received with the loudest acclamations of applause. It was indeed a reply to everything that had been said against the Address; but there was such an exquisite choice of expression and pronounced with such rapidity, that we were unable to do justice to any account we can give to it."

After several more meetings in York to rally voters, William returned to Hull to campaign in his old seat, which he would still need if things fell through in his bid to represent the whole of Yorkshire in Parliament. He need not have bothered. Two weeks later, canvassers in York announced that William Wilberforce and his running mate, Henry Duncombe, were four times more popular than any of the other candidates who supported Charles Fox. There was no need for an election: the Charles Fox supporters stepped aside and withdrew from the race. William Wilberforce and Henry Duncombe would be Yorkshire County's two representatives in the new Parliament. And with the win, William became the first ever merchant to hold the title of the Knight of the Shire for the County of Yorkshire.

Two days later, William received a letter from William Pitt. It began, "My dear Wilberforce, I can never enough congratulate you on such glorious success."

Chapter 7

Great Change

On May 14, 1784, William Wilberforce took up his new, powerful position in the House of Commons as representative for Yorkshire, the largest county in England. His success in the election had paved the way for William Pitt and his supporters to win a strong victory. Pitt remained prime minister, and this time the voters of Cambridge had elected him as their representative rather than his being the representative from the rotten borough of Appleby.

The first session of the new Parliament went well, and at every turn William supported William Pitt. Weekends were spent at Lauriston House, and when he hadn't been drinking too heavily the night before, William would attend the local Anglican church on Sunday morning. He found the service rather boring, not like Theophilus Lindsey's Unitarian congregation on Essex Street in London. This was a new type of church that many of the great thinkers of the day were attracted to. Unitarians did not believe in the Trinity or that Jesus preexisted His human birth. To them Jesus's life on earth was held up not as the way of salvation but as an example of how other human beings should live. William enjoyed listening to Lindsey preach, especially when Lindsey declared that reason and rational thought, science, and philosophy could all coexist with faith in God. That seemed to William a much firmer basis on which to live life.

In the fall, with winter on the horizon, William's mother wrote to say that William's sister Sally was not well. Neither were two of his cousins, Mary Bird and Bessy Smith. William's mother wondered if they would all be better off spending the winter on the European continent, where it would be warmer and drier. She asked William if he would consider escorting them there.

This sounded like a good idea to William. He had enjoyed his previous visit to France, even if two weeks of it were spent with the grocer in Rheims, and he wanted to see more of the country. The only problem he could foresee was the hundreds of hours they would spend sitting in coaches bumping along rutted roads on the way to the south of France. What he needed, William decided, was a male friend to go with him, someone who would be entertaining company on the journey.

William asked his friends in London and York, but everyone had other plans. Then, while attending the horse races in Scarborough, he saw Isaac

Milner, brother of his old schoolmaster in Hull. Isaac wasn't hard to recognize. He stood a full head above all the other spectators at the races, and William guessed that Isaac weighed at least three times what he weighed. Not only that, Isaac's booming Yorkshire accent carried across the crowd. The two men sat talking together for a long time. From time to time William had heard about Isaac's progress. Isaac had left Hull to attend Queen's College, Cambridge, where, because of his academic performance, he had been officially recognized at Cambridge University as *incomparabilis* (incomparable)—a genius. William knew that this was not a title bestowed lightly. Isaac had graduated first in mathematics and been elected a fellow of the Royal Society. Along with being a chemist and a mathematician, Isaac was a professor of natural philosophy at Cambridge and an ordained Anglican clergyman.

What made Isaac's accomplishments at Cambridge all the more amazing was that as a boy he had been apprenticed to a weaver and expected to spend the rest of his life behind a loom. The only reason he ever got to see anything besides the interior of a weaver's cottage was that a wealthy relative had sponsored his older brother, Joseph, to Cambridge, and Joseph had taken Isaac along with him as his personal servant. While serving his brother, Isaac discovered that he could learn better than many of the enrolled students at Cambridge.

William and Isaac both enjoyed telling jokes and stories, and the day passed quickly. Before they parted, William asked Isaac if he would like to accompany him on a trip to the Continent. The Cambridge professor agreed to go and set about securing a leave of absence from the university. Once it was granted, the group set off, crossing the English Channel to Calais on October 20, 1784. They took with them from England the coach in which the four women and their maid traveled, and William hired a chaise in France for him and Isaac to ride in.

Once in France they headed south to the French Riviera on the Mediterranean Sea. The trip of over a thousand miles from Yorkshire to Nice, where they planned to spend the winter, was bone-jarring.

Many other wealthy English people were spending the winter in Nice, and the Wilberforces and their companions soon settled into a continuous round of dinner parties, card games, and concerts. When Isaac joined in heartily, William watched to see whether, as an ordained clergyman, his friend would act in a religious manner. He saw no sign of that. It seemed to William that Isaac's faith was more theoretical than practical and did not seem to work itself out in the man's actions.

William's time in Nice was interrupted when he received a letter from William Pitt. The prime minister was about to introduce a reform bill to Parliament and needed William back in England to use his skills to help convince the House of Commons to pass the measure. William and Isaac decided to depart for England on February 5, 1785. Just as they were about to leave, William noticed a book his cousin Bessy had just finished reading. It was by Philip Doddridge and titled *The Rise and Progress of*

Religion in the Soul. He picked it up. "Is this worth reading?" he asked Isaac.

Isaac nodded. "Yes, it's one of the best books ever written. Let's take it with us and read it on our journey."

"If you think it would make for a good debate," William replied.

As they set out on the long coach ride back to Calais, Isaac began reading from the book, since William's poor eyesight strained his eyes even when he read sitting still in good light. There was no way his eyes would hold to read in a jostling coach.

"Chapter One," Isaac began.

> When we look around us with an attentive eye, and consider the characters and pursuits of men, we plainly see, that though, in the original constitution of their natures, they only, of all the creatures that dwell on the face of the earth, are capable of religion, yet many of them shamefully neglect it. And whatever different notions people may entertain of what they call religion, all must agree in owning that it is very far from being a universal thing. Religion, in its most general view, is such a Sense of God in the soul, and such a conviction of our obligations to him, and of our dependence upon him, as shall engage us to make it our great care to conduct ourselves in a manner which we have reason to believe will be pleasing to him.

On and on they read, with Isaac pausing at the end of most paragraphs to discuss their meaning and rereading those that were complicated. The weather grew colder as they approached the French Alps, and the two men wrapped themselves in woolen blankets as the landscape turned to a vista of snow and ice. Several times as they passed over the mountains, they had to get out of their chaise and walk beside it to lighten the load as the horses struggled to get their footing on the ice. It took eighteen days to reach Calais, from where they took a boat to Dover and continued on to London.

Once in London, William stayed awhile with William Pitt, who briefed him on the reform bill. Pitt explained that it was a modest bill that would introduce much-needed electoral reform in Great Britain. In essence the bill would remove representation from thirty-six rotten boroughs, freeing up seventy-two seats to be redistributed to the counties, to London, and to several of the important cities such as Bristol and Liverpool. William Pitt explained that he was going to introduce it as a Private Members' Bill, so that if it failed to pass, it would not bring down his government. He wanted William present in the Commons when he introduced the bill, and looked to him for support in trying to secure the necessary votes to pass it.

William, who also believed electoral reform was necessary, championed the bill as best he could. He tried to persuade individual members that they should support the bill, which he spoke eloquently and forcefully in favor of in the House of Commons.

But the bill had fierce opposition from Charles Fox and his supporters.

When not in Parliament, William spent his spare time attending the usual round of parties and dances. But in his diary he found himself writing strange thoughts and notions that he had not had before. After a dinner party he wrote about how odd it was to think that the pompous men being served and the waiters serving them would all end up standing before God, and that the lords and earls would not be any more important to God than the poorest servant. William realized that reading and discussing *The Rise and Progress of Religion in the Soul* with Isaac on their trip across France had deeply impacted his thinking. He was certain that the book had influenced Isaac's thinking as well. Their conversations about the meaning of what they read had been deep and soul-searching. In fact, while in London, William had secretly begun studying the New Testament in Greek, which he had learned while attending Pocklington School and had continued to study at Cambridge.

William stayed in London for four months, throwing his influence, intellect, and oratory skill behind the reform bill, but debate on the bill dragged on. In late June 1785, once again accompanied by Isaac Milner, William returned to the European continent. By now his mother, sister, and cousins had relocated to Genoa, Italy. Once in France, William and Isaac rented another chaise and set out for Italy.

It was another weary, bumpy coach ride as the men traveled on mile after mile. At night they would stay in dirty inns that served food both William and Isaac found hard to stomach. As they wound their way toward Italy, the two men resumed their conversation on Christianity, now using a Greek New Testament as their text, until they arrived in Genoa on July 11, just in time to escort the women to the city of Turin and then on to Geneva, Switzerland. On these journeys, William and Isaac sat in their chaise and engaged in more discussion of Christianity.

In September, their stay in Geneva over, the group traveled on to the town of Spa in the Austrian Netherlands (Belgium), where they stayed six weeks. In Spa, William was surprised to find that he did not enjoy partying and dancing with the other English visitors. He did go to see a play and spent his time there not looking at the actors on stage but looking at the wealthy audience. He wondered how they could enjoy a play when there was so much suffering back home in England. Again William was shocked by his thoughts. A year ago he had been an enthusiastic theatergoer, and now he knew those times were over.

Other changes were taking place. William began to get up early each morning to spend the first hour of the day alone thinking. He wrote in his diary that he hoped this would make some kind of difference in his life. It did make a difference, but not the one William expected. As he thought and meditated in the mornings, William soon concluded that he was a sinner before God. He felt guilty and depressed. The verse from the New Testament book of James, chapter four, verse seventeen, "Therefore to him that knoweth to do good, and doeth it not, to him it is sin," jumped out at him. Somewhere along his rambling journey in Europe, William Wilberforce had become convinced that Christianity was true, and now he felt miserable—more miserable than he had ever before felt in his life.

William wondered what this change of heart would mean for him. Could he possibly go on in Parliament, debating bills, arguing with the opposition, even mocking them? Could he continue attending the endless round of balls, parties, and concerts in London or remain the best friend of the prime minister, with whom he'd had so many conversations about the narrow-mindedness of Methodists and other religious do-gooders? William didn't think so.

While still in Spa, William received a letter from William Pitt, who declared that he was looking forward to William's return to England, that the reform bill seemed destined for defeat in Parliament, and that his sister Harriot had married Edward Eliot, one of their best friends, on September 24, 1785. William was delighted by the news of the marriage. He couldn't think of a better match. He looked forward to getting home and wishing them a long and happy marriage.

In early November the traveling party returned to England. Although William was glad to be home, once settled again in London he was restless and worried. His views on so many things had changed, and he was sure he could not go back to the House of Commons. Was it even possible for a Christian—especially one with Methodist leanings—to be an effective politician?

William was convinced it wasn't possible and knew he needed to tell William Pitt what had happened to him before Pitt heard about it from someone else. But he worried about the effect the news might have on his friend. Still, on November 24, 1785, William sat down and wrote one of the hardest letters he'd ever written. In it he explained that he had become a Christian, which was in itself awkward, since all of the members of Parliament belonged to the Church of England and all called England a Christian nation. Then he talked about how he wanted to resign from Parliament and seek to live a life of solitude where he could study the Bible and pray all day.

William's hands shook as he handed the letter to his servant to mail. Now he was thoroughly miserable. Turning his heart toward God had not made him happy but had caused him to be tormented. He needed someone to talk to. As he searched his mind for who might understand his predicament, he recalled the old captain of a slave ship turned Christian minister—John Newton. The moment William thought of him, he knew he was the one he should visit. Newton was now sixty years old and rector at St. Mary Woolnoth Church in London, where he had a huge following.

William knew that if he was seen with John Newton, or even sitting in his church, rumors would fly and questions would be asked. He wasn't sure he was strong enough to handle that. Still, the idea of unburdening himself to the old sea captain would not go away. On December 2 William wrote him a letter stating, "I wish to have some serious conversation with you. . . . I have had ten thousand doubts within myself, whether or not I should discover [unburden] myself to you; but every argument against doing it has its foundation in pride. I am sure you will hold yourself bound to let no one living know of this application [request], or of my visit."

Just as he finished writing the letter, a messenger arrived with a reply from William Pitt. William's hands trembled as he opened it. Would his best friend mock him for what he had done? William scanned the letter, stopping from time to time to ponder William Pitt's words.

> Believe me it is impossible that it should shake the sentiments of affection and friendship which I bear towards you. . . . They are sentiments engraved on my heart, and will never be effaced or weakened. . . . But forgive me if I cannot help expressing my fear that you are nevertheless deluding yourself into principles which have but too much tendency to counteract your own object, and to render your virtues and your talents useless both to yourself and mankind. . . . The only way you can satisfy me is by conversation. There ought to be no awkwardness or embarrassment to either of us.

William Pitt ended his letter with, "Believe me, affectionately and unalterably yours, W Pitt."

Tears welled in William's eyes as he read the letter. It was clear from the long letter that his best friend and the prime minister of Great Britain wanted him to stay on in Parliament and use his newfound religious principles to do good there. It was not the response William had expected, and he found himself more conflicted than ever. Was his place now in a cottage in the Lake District, studying and praying like a monk, or was it in the most public of places, the House of Commons, arguing and meeting with ungodly men? William had no idea what he should do and was more convinced than ever that he needed to talk with John Newton.

Two days later, on Sunday, December 4, 1785, William decided to deliver the letter himself to John Newton's house. He handed it to the servant who opened the door and waited for a reply, which soon arrived. Newton was unable to see him right then, but he would be happy to arrange a meeting on Wednesday. William could hardly wait. So many thoughts and plans were racing through his mind that he could not sleep.

On Wednesday, when William arrived at Newton's house, he lacked the courage to knock on the door. So much was at stake. If anyone saw him coming or going, the gossip would be brutal, and William was sure he would lose all respect in the House of Commons. After walking around the square outside Newton's home several times, he screwed up his courage, climbed the front steps, and knocked. John Newton greeted him at the door, and the two men were soon seated inside, deep in conversation.

William was relieved to be able to describe to Newton what he had been going through, how slowly and unevenly his conversion, or "great change," as he liked to call it, had happened. Newton nodded and listened quietly until William got to the part where he said he thought it was his duty to quit politics and follow God.

"Are you sure that is necessary?" Newton asked at that point. "It does not seem to me that you must leave one to embark upon the other. It is possible that the Lord wants you to be both a Christian and a statesman. Although these roles do not often exist together, they are not incompatible."

William felt his body relax. Here was a deeply Christian man telling him he should not abandon politics but use his position to do good in the name of God. It was the same thing William Pitt had told him in his letter several days before. Perhaps, William concluded, his life, far from being private and dedicated to God, was about to become a very public display of what God could do through a man. The thought both thrilled and terrified him. Staying in Parliament would take just as much—if not more—courage as walking away from it. That much William was sure of. What he wasn't sure of was what would happen next. Surely, if God wanted him to stay in politics, He must have some reason—some cause that he should take up. But what was it?

Chapter 8

The Obvious Choice

Through fresh eyes William began to see the society in which he lived, and he didn't like what he saw. In the words of St. Paul, sin abounded. The poor drank cheap gin to escape their miserable lives, while the rich drank claret to celebrate theirs. Poor children as young as four years old worked sixteen hours a day in coal mines and factories, and rich young men gambled away their inheritances at the clubs. The Sabbath Day rest was broken, and people thought nothing of swearing and dueling to the death on a Sunday or on any day. The punishments for crime were barbaric—hangings, burnings, deportations to far-off Australia. What was needed, William concluded, was a fresh start.

In his reading, William had come across a proclamation made by the British king and queen, William and Mary, when they ascended to the throne in 1692. In their royal proclamation the monarchs called for the promotion of virtue and suppression of vice among their subjects. According to the history books William read, the proclamation and the association that was formed around it had a positive impact on society. It seemed to him that what England needed now was another royal proclamation and a new association to reform people's morals, or manners, as they were called. William set to work on organizing this. Many prominent men, including the archbishop of Canterbury, worked quietly with him to help bring it about.

Before the summer recess, William got the opportunity to bring his first bills before Parliament. *I have to start somewhere. It might as well be with dead bodies,* he thought as he studied a newspaper article included in the package he had recently received. The article from the *Times* referred to Phoebe Harris, a woman who'd been executed and her remains burned in public view outside Newgate Prison days earlier. Her crime was coining—making counterfeit coins. The newspaper reporter wrote,

> The execution of a woman for coining on Wednesday morning, reflects a scandal upon the law and was not only inhuman, but shamefully indelicate and shocking. Why should the law in this species of offence inflict a severer punishment upon a woman, than a man? It is not an offence which she can perpetrate alone—in every such case the insistence of

> a man has been found the operating motive upon the woman; yet the man is but hanged, and the woman [also] burned.

William scanned the other newspaper articles in the package, which he'd been expecting from Dr. Hey, a well-respected surgeon from Leeds in Yorkshire. Dr. Hey had asked William to introduce a bill into Parliament that would stop the burning of the bodies of executed female prisoners. The bill would also allow for more of the bodies of executed men and women to be used in medical schools for education, a provision that promised to cut down on the procurement of bodies through illegal means, a source of further violence and crime.

William didn't like to think about these topics, but he felt it was his Christian duty to do what he could to curb violence. He introduced the bill, which passed the House of Commons. To his astonishment, however, members of the House of Lords argued against it. Lord Loughborough, as chief justice, took a particular exception to the bill. He argued that the public burnings were a great way to leave a strong impression on the crowd about the perils of committing serious offenses. William disagreed. He felt that those who came to watch such a thing were hurt by it. The brutality involved dulled their sense of kindness and goodness. And in the end, that would lead to a weaker, less moral society.

It was hard for William to believe that he had to argue about such things with so-called civilized men. It was even harder for him to accept that his bill had failed to pass in the House of Lords. Changing the law to promote better morals was going to be harder than William had first imagined.

William's other bill did not fare any better. It was a registration bill that sought to register all eligible voters so that they could vote where they lived instead of having to return to their home voting stations. The registration bill passed in the House of Commons, but it too got hung up in the House of Lords, where it failed to pass. However, William wasn't too sad about the outcome, since he had come to believe that the bill had some serious flaws, and he was relieved when it did not pass in the Lords.

This was not a great beginning to William's new Christian political life, and in early July, William was glad to escape London, even though it meant visiting his mother and sister in Scarborough for summer vacation.

While William's mother had been present with him in Europe as he underwent his "great change," he had never spoken to her about it. By now he was aware that his mother knew of his Christian stand and how he had resigned from all five of the social clubs where he had spent so much time in London. It was hard for William to imagine that she would be any happier about this now than when he first became involved in Methodist Christianity through his aunt Hannah and uncle William. But William reminded himself that he had been a nine-year-old boy then. Now he was a grown man of twenty-six and in charge of his own destiny.

William need not have been concerned. His mother was impressed with how much he had changed. She told William he was more patient and kind to her than he had ever been before. Even their family friend Mrs. Sykes, who was vacationing with them, commented, "If this is madness, I hope that he will bite us all."

After a pleasant stay at the seaside in Scarborough, the Wilberforces traveled to Nottingham to stay with their Smith relatives. Here William began his new study habit. As he reflected on his life, he was upset about the time and opportunities he had wasted while at Cambridge. Now he determined to make up for it. He had brought a bag of books, which he started to study for ten hours a day. He read history, literature, economics, philosophy, and science and memorized large portions of the Bible.

William was still in Nottingham in September when he received a letter telling him that Harriot Eliot, William Pitt's sister and the wife of his friend Edward Eliot, had died after giving birth to a daughter. Harriot, only twenty-eight years old, had been smart and witty like her brother, and William was heartbroken over her death. He prayed for Pitt, especially since his only other sister had died from the same cause. He wrote to a mutual friend about it. "How can we go on as if present things were to last for ever, when so often reminded by accidents like these, 'that the fashion of this world passes away!' Every day I live I see greater reason in considering this life but as a passage to another."

The following month William was back in Hull with his mother when he received another letter. This one was a startling request from Sir Charles Middleton, the father-in-law of William's Cambridge friend Gerard Edwards. Sir Charles was also the comptroller of the Royal Navy, an authority on farming, and a member of the House of Commons. Since becoming a Christian, William had come to know Sir Charles and his wife, Lady Margaret Middleton, well. The Middletons were both staunch Methodists, and William visited them often in their London home.

In his letter Sir Charles said that a number of interesting people had gathered at Barham Court, his country estate in Teston, Kent, to discuss what could be done about abolishing slavery in the British West Indian sugar colonies. Beilby Porteus, the bishop of London, was there, as were Benjamin La Trobe, the leader of the Moravians, the only missionary group working among the slaves, and a young man from Cambridge, Thomas Clarkson. Sir Charles related that as the group conversed, they decided that what their cause needed most of all was a spokesperson in Parliament. Although Sir Charles was a member of the House of Commons, he explained in his letter that he did not like to speak publicly and that William Pitt did not like him. The obvious choice to be the group's spokesperson, Sir Charles concluded, was none other than William Wilberforce.

William laid down the letter and stared at it for a long time. He thought back to his two attempts at bringing bills before Parliament. Both had failed. And one of those bills, targeted at stopping a public spectacle of violence, had seemed so obviously right. He had thought that on purely humanitarian grounds the bill would have passed. But the opposition to his bill in the House of Lords had surprised and saddened him. And now he was being asked to lead an effort to get these same men to pass a bill abolishing slavery. That didn't seem a likely outcome to William. Parliament was made up of rich men, most of whom had some tie to and gained some wealth from the slave trade. Why would these men support any bill that tried to interfere with their money supply?

William wondered how anyone was supposed to battle slavery. After all, King George III and the Church of England both had large amounts of money invested in trade with the West Indies. And a large number of bishops sat in the House of Lords. William shook his head. This was a much bigger fight than he felt capable of taking on. It would take years, and there was no guarantee of success even then. William pondered the careful reply he would need to draft in response to the letter. He didn't want to discourage the efforts of the others, but he hesitated to commit himself to such a challenging cause. At last he wrote in reply, "I feel the great importance of the subject, though I think myself unequal to the task allotted to me. However, I would not positively decline the offer, and when I return to London I will pay you a visit in Teston and consult with you."

Over the next few days William recalled his various exposures to the cause of the abolition of slavery. He vaguely remembered writing an essay on the subject when he was a student at Pocklington School. And he certainly remembered as a boy listening to John Newton tell him stories about life and conditions on slave ships. In addition, when William had run for a seat in the House of Commons the first time back in Hull, his opponent was the eccentric

David Hartley. In 1776 Hartley had put the matter of slavery before the House of Commons, saying, "The slave trade is contrary to the laws of God and the rights of men." The bill Hartley put forward sought to end the slave trade and was easily defeated. When William beat Hartley in the election, he had assured his opponent that if the opportunity arose, he would keep the matter of ending slavery alive in Parliament. William wondered why he had even said that. He certainly hadn't done anything about it since.

William also thought of the dinner party he had attended three years before at the home of Edward and Diana Edwards. He recalled another guest who was there that night, a man named James Ramsay. The Reverend Ramsay had woven a fascinating tale about how in 1759 he had been a surgeon aboard HMS *Arundel* in the West Indies under the command of Sir Charles Middleton. The *Arundel* had come up beside a British slave ship named the *Swift*, which had been captured by a French ship the day before. The French had soon learned that there was dysentery aboard, and they had taken the still healthy slaves to sell and abandoned the other one hundred slaves.

Ramsay had bravely boarded the *Swift* and was met with the most horrific sight of his life. Dead bodies lay chained in tight rows, next to the dying, and the slaves still alive begged for water. Ramsay did what he could for them before returning to the *Arundel*, where he had tripped and broken his thighbone. He had become lame and had to resign his position as surgeon. That was when he decided to become a

Church of England clergyman. He studied in England and then returned to the West Indies, where he worked among the plantation owners and their slaves for fifteen years before going back to Great Britain, where he stayed with Sir Charles and Lady Margaret Middleton and eventually became the vicar at Teston, Kent.

William thought also about the court case heard in London in 1783 that highlighted the inhumanity of the slave trade. The case was over an incident that had happened aboard the slave ship *Zong* near Jamaica two years before. The ship had been carrying 442 slaves from Africa to Jamaica when the captain fell ill and the crew made a navigational error that sent them sailing right by Jamaica. When the crew realized their error, they turned the *Zong* around and headed back to Jamaica, several days' sail away. By then water aboard ship was running low, and a decision was made to throw about 140 of the slaves overboard. The ship's owners had insurance to cover the loss of "cargo" jettisoned to save the ship and so made a claim for insurance to cover their loss. When the insurance company refused to pay, a court ruled in favor of the owners and ordered the insurers to cover the loss of the jettisoned slaves.

In 1783, new evidence came to light, and another trial was held in London. It turned out that after the first forty-two slaves had been thrown overboard, it had rained heavily, replenishing the *Zong*'s water supply. Despite this, the crew of the ship had continued to throw slaves overboard to drown. The new evidence led to the earlier ruling being overturned so that the insurance company no longer had to pay out on the loss. The evidence presented at the second court case galvanized many people to action. A group of Quakers presented a petition to Parliament containing nearly three hundred signatures calling for the abolition of the slave trade.

Granville Sharp, a tenacious legal fighter, had taken on the task of attempting to have the crew of the *Zong* tried for murder. Sharp had tried several important cases relating to slaves in the past and had earned a reputation as the "protector of the Negro." One of the cases he defended was that of James Somerset, a slave from the Virginia colony in North America who had been taken to England with his master in 1769 and had run away in 1771. The case produced an important result. Somerset was caught fifty-six days after running away and was put on a ship for Jamaica, where his master intended to sell him. However, a court hearing ensued before he left England in which Granville Sharp and several other lawyers argued the slave's side. In the end, Lord Mansfield, Chief Justice of the King's Bench, ruled in favor of Somerset, acknowledging that English law did not allow slavery, and only an Act of Parliament could make it legal. Since there was no such act, Somerset could not be forcibly removed from England and sent back to a life of servitude.

As much as William admired Granville Sharp, he also pitied him. Sharp was always fighting mammoth legal battles, and he lost as many cases as he won. That was what had happened in the case of the *Zong*. Despite Sharp's best efforts, no crew member of the slave ship was ever charged with murder or any other crime for the killing of the 140 slaves aboard the *Zong*.

On his way back to London in November 1786, William thought and prayed about what he should do next. So many things that had seemed important no longer interested him. Lauriston House was one of those things. Once he had loved entertaining his Goostree's Club friends there at all-night parties. Now the upkeep of the house and the need to hire enough servants to run it for just one person to live in part-time seemed a waste of money. William decided that he would sell the house and find a smaller place in London close to Parliament.

By now William had become reacquainted with his aunt Hannah and her half brother and William's cousin, John Thornton. John invited William to spend time at his new home at Clapham Common anytime he wanted. This suited William fine. He was glad to be welcomed back into John and Aunt Hannah's circle of Christian friends and planned to take up the offer to spend time with the Thorntons at Clapham.

Once back in London, William found himself a new home. It was a smaller, two-story stone house at 4 Old Palace Yard and was right across the street from the king's entrance to the House of Lords. The location suited William well. It meant that he now had a base in London from which he could invite people to dine with him rather than accompanying them to the various clubs he used to belong to.

In early January 1787, after settling into his new home, a stranger appeared at William's door. He was a tall, redheaded man, and he carried a letter of introduction from Sir Charles Middleton. The man was Thomas Clarkson, an abolitionist who was about to turn William Wilberforce's world upside down.

Chapter 9

Take Up the Fight

A servant showed Thomas Clarkson into the library, where Thomas and William drank tea together as they talked. It was obvious to William his guest was a man on a mission.

"It all started, for me at least, at Cambridge two years ago. I understand you went to St. John's as well?" Thomas said.

"I did," William said, thinking what a different kind of student this intense man sitting in his library must have been. "But I do not recall you being there."

"Although we are the same age, I didn't begin attending St. John's College until 1779, the year you left, I believe. You, sir, have made a strong beginning on a career, and I am lagging." Then he added with a smile, "Well, more than lagging. I have abandoned any hope of one. But I am getting ahead of myself." Thomas took a sip of tea and continued. "In my final year at Cambridge, Professor Peckard, the vice-chancellor, set an essay topic for a competition. The topic was *Anne liceat invitos in servitutem dare*?"

"Is it lawful to enslave those who do not consent?" William asked, translating out loud from the Latin. "An interesting topic."

"Indeed," Thomas replied, his eyes lighting up. "I must confess to becoming quite engrossed in it. It led me to consider the question of slavery—something I had no interest in or knowledge of before. In writing the essay I read everything I could find on the subject. I found the works of Anthony Benezet to be particularly helpful. He was the American who roused his fellow Quakers to call for the freedom of slaves in the colony of Pennsylvania. I also sought out every person I could find with firsthand information on the subject."

William watched as Thomas bent down and reached into his satchel.

"This is what I found," Thomas said, placing a stack of slim leather-bound notebooks on a side table. "Recorded in these are the stories of sea captains and sailors who have seen the vile trade firsthand."

"Impressive," William said. "I take it you made a good showing in the essay competition?"

"I won it," Thomas said, "and I thought that was the end of it. But the facts I learned gripped me and would not let me go. When I graduated, I planned to be a clergyman like my father, but as I was riding to London to take up my first post, I stopped near Ware in Hertfordshire and could not go on. A thought came to my mind and would not leave: 'I have written an essay, but the essay speaks of the most cruel destiny of millions of fellow human beings. Before I wrote I could have dismissed the facts as embroidered, but I have heard the stories with my own ears, I have written them with my own pen, they are here.'" Thomas patted the stack of leather-bound notebooks.

"As you can imagine," Thomas continued, "I was in quite a state. I dismounted my horse, and holding his reins I sat disconsolate at the side of the road. Then another thought came to me: 'If the content of the essay is true—which I believe it to be—someone has to commit himself to ending slavery.' By God's grace I have done nothing else since that day but focus on its end."

William sat in silence. What could he say? Sitting in his library was a passionate young man who had, apparently, committed his life to the goal of ending slavery. "Are you alone, or have you attracted companions?" William asked.

"It is as if the hand of God is gathering us up," Thomas replied, his eyes sparkling.

"Oh?" William said, realizing now that his visitor probably imagined him playing a role in this extraordinary undertaking.

"When I came to London, I had difficulty finding anyone who would publish my essay, until I spoke to a stranger in the street. He turned out to be James Phillips, the Quaker bookseller, and he willingly published my work. He then introduced me to Granville Sharp, James Ramsay, and William Dillwyn, who, you may recall, presented to Parliament the petition with its three hundred Quaker signatures calling for the end of slavery. James Ramsay introduced me to Sir Charles Middleton, who suggested I call on you. Here, I have brought you a copy of the essay." Thomas reached into his satchel again. This time he pulled out a booklet and handed it to William.

"An essay on the slavery and commerce of the human species, particularly the African, translated from a Latin dissertation," William read aloud from the cover.

"May I be so bold as to suggest you read it, Mr. Wilberforce, and that I return this time next week to further our discussion?"

William looked hard at Thomas. He felt sure that if he said yes he would be drawn into the man's scheme to end slavery. It was such a grandiose plan, so challenging a goal, but something in William resonated with Thomas's ambition. "You may call again, Mr. Clarkson," he said, "and by then, I hope to have read your essay. We can discuss it at that time."

"Very well," Thomas replied, putting the notebooks back into his satchel. "Shall I see you at the same time?"

"Yes, certainly," William said, standing and shaking hands with the visitor.

After Thomas had left, William stood holding the essay and wondering what he had let himself in for.

Throughout the next few weeks, Thomas Clarkson introduced William to a scattered group of people: Quakers, lawyers, clergymen, a theater patroness, even a freed slave who had been kidnapped in Africa, traveled the known world in a British ship, and settled in England a free man. William thought they were a fascinating group, yet he was cautious. He was sure the reason Thomas visited him each week and introduced him to these people was so that he would be drawn into the antislavery cause, to be its most public face and spokesperson in Parliament.

On March 13, 1787, William found himself at a meeting of a large group of antislavery people gathered at the home of writer Bennet Langton. At the meeting Thomas Clarkson asked William publicly if he would represent the cause in Parliament. William wasn't ready to answer the question directly, but he did say he would consider it if no one better could be found.

William had his doubts about taking up the challenge, and he talked with the two people he trusted most, John Newton and William Pitt. John Newton, who was slowly writing an account of his years as a slave ship captain, urged William to take up the cause. He wrote advising him, "God has raised you up for the good of the church and the good of the nation; maintain your friendship with Pitt, continue in Parliament, who knows that but for such a time as this God has brought you into public life and has a purpose for you."

On May 12, 1787, William visited William Pitt at his country estate, Holwood. Pitt's cousin, William Grenville, was also visiting. The three young men, each aged twenty-seven, took a walk together. They began discussing the slave trade, and William confessed that he was getting a lot of pressure to be the spokesperson for the cause in Parliament.

After climbing to the top of a steep slope, the three men stopped beneath a huge spreading oak tree. As they rested, William Pitt told William, "This is an undertaking you are perfectly suited to. All of your talents and character are in line with taking up the issue of slavery. No one else in the House of Commons has your passion, or your reputation. What's more, you serve Yorkshire, one of the few counties in the country with few direct ties to the slave trade. I imagine you will gain the support of a great many of your constituents." He paused for a moment to pick a daffodil and then carried on. "Do not lose time, or someone else, less suited than you, will take up the fight."

William knew that his friend was speaking the truth. It was time to throw his hat in with the abolitionists. "All right. I shall be their man in Parliament," he declared. "I will give notice at the first fit occasion in the House of Commons that I will bring the subject forward."

William Pitt clapped William on the back. "You will have my full support, as always, though you know I will have to play a political game while you press forward in earnest."

Ten days later, Thomas Clarkson visited William to tell him that an official Committee for the Abolition of the Slave Trade had been formed. It consisted of twelve men, nine Quakers and three members of the Church of England. It was a good balance. Although Quakers, along with the Moravians, were the earliest group to speak against slavery, they could not be elected to Parliament. The inclusion of the three Anglicans, Granville Sharp, Thomas Clarkson, and Philip Sansom, gave the committee a greater legitimacy.

The committee started with a burst of energy. Their ultimate goal was the abolition of British involvement in slavery anywhere in the world. Granville Sharp pointed out that if they targeted the right of an Englishman to own a slave anywhere in the world, it would become a huge constitutional issue. Supporters of slavery would argue that Parliament had no authority over their private property in a foreign colony. But no one could argue with the right of Parliament to regulate British trade, and transporting an African to a colony was an act of trade. As a result, the committee members decided to break their goal into smaller, more manageable pieces.

Following Granville's suggestion, the committee settled on first ending the slave trade, making it illegal to purchase kidnapped Africans and transport them halfway around the world to plantations, where they were worked to death. The committee also hoped that if the supply of "fresh" slaves from Africa was cut off, plantation owners in the Caribbean would take better care of the slaves they did have. This would give the committee time to obtain enough parliamentary support to end slavery throughout the British Empire altogether.

Although William was not a member of the committee, he was in constant contact with Granville and Thomas. Together they decided not to make their aims public right away. Thomas could then tour England and collect reports and statements from sailors, captains, doctors, and former slaves before the public knew what the committee intended to do with these reports and statements. Thomas's work would then become a lot more difficult and dangerous.

William arranged for Thomas to have access to all the shipping records the government kept at the Customs House. From these records Thomas hoped to be able to give reliable numbers of slaves and sailors who died during the "Middle Passage." The Middle Passage referred to the voyage of a slave ship from Africa across the Atlantic Ocean to the Caribbean and North America. When a slave ship left England for the west coast of Africa, it would depart loaded with manufactured goods. These goods would be traded for kidnapped Africans, who were then loaded onto the ship and transported across the Atlantic as slaves. Once the ship reached the slave markets in the Caribbean and North America, the slaves were sold or traded for raw materials that would fetch a high price in Great Britain. The ship, laden with such raw materials, would then head back to England, completing a triangular voyage. The second leg of this journey, where the slaves were carried aboard ship, was the Middle Passage.

Thomas agreed to take to his friend Josiah Wedgewood the newly adopted symbol of the committee, a picture of a black man kneeling in chains, with the words "Am I not a man and a brother?" written around him. Josiah owned a successful pottery in Stoke-on-Trent and had declared himself for abolition. The committee hoped that he would make some medallions for them based on the picture and donate them to the cause.

It was left to William to figure out the best way to work within Parliament. Five other evangelical Christians in the House of Commons had told William that they would support his reformation of morals and his bid to end slavery. The men were Sir Charles Middleton; Walter Spencer-Stanhope, whose family had made a fortune in the iron trade; and William Wilberforce's distant cousins, the brothers Henry, Robert, and Samuel Thornton. William had grown especially close to Henry and had influenced him to follow in the footsteps of his father, John Thornton, as a dedicated Christian.

Meanwhile, William's other idea, the reformation of morals, was gaining public attention. On June 1, 1787, King George III issued a proclamation based on earlier royal proclamations, titled "For the Encouragement of Piety and Virtue and for the Preventing and Punishing of Vice, Profaneness and Immorality." This circumstance had come about because of William's friend, Beilby Porteus, the bishop of London, who had been the king's personal chaplain. Bishop Porteus had encouraged the king to make the proclamation, in which King George stated that all "persons of honor and authority" must set a good example of moral living. The king also proclaimed the end of gambling on Sunday and called for the prosecution of anyone who drank excessively, blasphemed, swore, or cursed, along with a long list of other vices. He made it clear that these matters were now law and would be enforced by sheriffs and judges in every county.

William believed that such reforms would go a long way in making England a safer and better place. He planned to spend his summer traveling throughout England encouraging the formation of proclamation societies to carry out the king's orders. William imagined these societies being led by prominent people who would make reforming morals fashionable.

Throughout the summer, William crisscrossed the country encouraging lords and prominent merchants to start proclamation societies. During his travels he stayed in touch with Thomas and other members of the Committee for the Abolition of the Slave Trade. By summer's end, he was exhausted. A doctor told him that he was not taking proper care of himself and that he should eat a lot of meat and drink more wine if he hoped to grow strong and not lose his eyesight. The doctor also suggested that he bathe in the mineral waters at Bath. William was glad to go to Bath, where the More sisters lived.

William had been introduced to Hannah More by Sir Charles. Hannah was one of five sisters who were all educated by their schoolmaster father. The sisters decided not to marry and instead start their own school together. Although Hannah was the third sister, she was the natural leader, and William was fascinated by her wit and intelligence. Hannah confided to William that she was taking her Christian faith more seriously lately and encouraged William in his work. She was a well-known writer and offered to write a book about the manners and morals of the rich and privileged. William thought this an excellent idea.

Bathing in the mineral baths did make William feel better, and he headed back to London for the winter session of Parliament feeling optimistic and refreshed. On October 25, 1787, he wrote in his journal, "God Almighty has set before me two great objects: the suppression of the slave trade and the reformation of manners [morals]." Both causes were moving forward at a great speed.

In December, just after Christmas, William Wilberforce stood to speak in the House of Commons. The time had come for action. "Early in the new year, I shall put forward a motion for the abolition of the slave trade," he declared boldly.

William had no way of knowing that by then he would be fighting for his life.

Chapter 10

"We Are All Guilty"

William lay in bed, his body wet from fever. Through the fog in his mind he could hear whispering. A female voice said, "We're here. We came as soon as we could. What is to be done for him?" A male voice replied, "Not much. He's seen Dr. Pitcairne, the best doctor in London. He says William has ulcers throughout his stomach. I've been making him as comfortable as possible, but he's lost a lot of weight and he can't eat. Dr. Warren, who has also been consulted, says his guts are shot through and he cannot last long."

William lost focus on the conversation and drifted off to sleep. He awoke an hour later, his mother and sister sitting at his bedside. His mother dabbed his forehead with a damp cloth. "How do you feel?" she asked.

All William could do was nod. He was too weak to speak.

For the next week, doctors, friends, and family drifted in and out of William's consciousness. Sometimes William knew who a person was, other times he did not. But he did know that he was ill and, from the snippets of conversation he overheard, learned he was not expected to live long. He even heard that an opposing candidate in Yorkshire was gearing up to take his place as the county representative in Parliament when he died.

Isaac Milner rushed to William's side to help in any way he could. He explained that when he had heard of William's illness, he canceled his lectures and came straight to London. William's mother, his sister Sally, and Isaac took turns spooning watery soup into William's mouth. Sometimes William kept it down, but his stomach felt as though it was on fire as he digested it. Dr. Pitcairne visited him regularly and prescribed medicine to calm his stomach and save his life.

Bit by bit, the treatment was effective, and William began to recover from his illness. Whenever he felt well enough, his thoughts went to the bill to abolish the slave trade he was supposed to be preparing to present to Parliament in a few weeks. He tried to work on the bill but found he could not concentrate for long.

In early April 1788, past the time when he should have been speaking in Parliament, William felt well enough to travel to Bath for the recommended bathing therapy. Before he left, William Pitt visited him and promised he would take up the anti-slave-trade bill himself. William was grateful that his friend would take such a risky political stand on his behalf. The two men discussed strategy. In February William Pitt had commissioned the Privy Council committee for trade and foreign plantations to study and produce a report on the slave trade and its effects on and consequences for British commerce. In the meantime, the prime minister would raise the issue of the slave trade in Parliament at the beginning of May by putting forward a motion that would call for the House of Commons, early in the next session, to consider the circumstances of the slave trade. He hoped that by then the Privy Council would have produced its report, which could form the basis of discussion in Parliament, and that by then William would be well enough to return to the House of Commons to steer the debate.

Following the visit, William headed west to Bath, where he stayed a month, drinking the mineral water and bathing in it. When the month was up, Isaac took William back to Cambridge to rest some more.

Once at Cambridge, through letters and reports, William was able to follow what was happening in Parliament. And there was a lot to keep up with. On May 9, 1788, as promised, William Pitt stood in the House of Commons and proposed a resolution that in the next session the chamber officially begin investigating the slave trade. No one objected. No one spoke against the measure, and the resolution passed. This was good news on the surface, but William Wilberforce was certain that the anti-abolitionist faction would not take it lying down. It would not be that easy to get the measure passed in Parliament. The anti-abolitionists would await the right time to attack. And that time came on May 26, when William Dolben, the member of Parliament for Oxford, put forward a bill that sought to regulate the number of slaves a ship could carry based upon the vessel's reported tonnage. Dolben had been moved to take this action after visiting a slave ship docked in London, where he found conditions aboard deplorable.

Through subsequent debate on the bill, it was learned that between 5 and 10 percent of all slaves transported on slaves ships died during the Middle Passage. What was worse, on some vessels, up to one-third of all the slaves being transported perished.

From Cambridge, William admired Dolben's pluck in introducing a bill that sought to regulate some aspect of the slave trade. But his heart sank at the swift and sharp attack of the anti-abolitionists on the bill. Shipowners in Liverpool, where many of the companies involved in the slave trade were based, claimed that the crowded quarters on their ships during the Middle Passage were actually more healthy and comforting for the Africans, who liked being close together. Others argued that any regulation passed by Parliament that put restrictions on British slave traders would simply put money into the hands of the French, their archrivals in the Caribbean slave trade. They were sure that this was not what the government wanted, especially since the king of France and his government were mired in a deepening political crisis.

William Pitt tired of such arguments and found them absurd and inhumane. William Wilberforce read in the newspaper how his friend rose to his feet in the House of Commons to rebut them. William nodded in assent as he read how William Pitt declared that the slave trade was "shocking to humanity" and "abominable to be carried on by any country." Pitt went on to point out the dishonor that Great Britain's involvement in the slave trade brought upon the nation. "The Trade, as the petitioners propose to carry it on, without any regulation, is contrary to every humane, to every Christian principle, to every sentiment that ought to inspire the breast of man." William wished he could have been present in the House to encourage and support his friend.

Pitt's words seemed to quiet the opposition for the time being, and the Slave Trade Act, as Dolben's bill was officially known, passed in the House of Commons on June 18, 1788, and then the House of Lords in early July. It was the first parliamentary legislation passed to regulate conditions on British slave ships.

As William continued his slow recovery, he moved from Cambridge to Rayrigg, his rented cottage in the Lake District. He gained enough strength to row a boat out onto the lake early in the mornings, pull it up on one of the lake's islands, and pray and read his Bible, doing it all within the shadow of the majestic surrounding mountains.

By November, nine months after he became ill, William felt well enough to return to London and Parliament. Once back in London, he hoped to make quick work of getting a bill authorizing the abolition of the slave trade passed through Parliament. But something got in the way—King George III went mad.

"Yes, apparently he's quite mad," William Pitt told William quietly. "I have reports of him standing on a table at dinner, yelling to the moon and frothing at the mouth."

"What can be done about it?" William asked.

"The usual. Doctors believe that his Majesty is suffering from gout and that it has flown from his feet to his head and lodged there. They have shaved his head and are applying hot disks to blister his scalp and draw the gout out of his body."

"I see," William said. "How long can this go on before it becomes a constitutional crisis?"

"About another hour," William Pitt said dryly. "I hear the Prince of Wales is already scheming with Charles Fox on how to become regent for the king."

Both Williams knew that this would be bad for the country. As regent, the Prince of Wales, the king's oldest son, would rule in place of his father, at least until the king either got better or died, at which time the prince would become king in his own right. King George III, at least when he was sane, was a moral man. He was faithful to his wife, he read the Bible to his daughters every night before bed, and he prayed regularly for himself and his country.

The king's oldest son, the Prince of Wales, was the exact opposite. He was notoriously immoral, he drank heavily and was often drunk, and he gambled away large sums of money. As well, in league with Charles Fox, he was hungry for political power.

William knew that when or if the prince became regent or king, he would most certainly dismiss William Pitt, whom he disliked, as prime minister and call for a new election. William was certain that that would stall any hope of passing a bill to end Britain's involvement in the slave trade. Without the backing and support in Parliament of someone as important and politically savvy as William Pitt, such a bill was doomed. Even with Pitt's support, it was going to be a tough fight. William was also concerned about his reformation of morals campaign. Despite the formation of societies around the country, this campaign still depended on royal support, support he knew he would not get if the Prince of Wales became regent or king.

By the end of November, the two Williams' fears were being realized. The royal family was moved from Windsor Castle to a house at Kew that had a private garden where the king could rave without being seen by passersby. By now the king was screaming foul language at his wife, Queen Charlotte, trying to assault the maids, and imagining he could see what was happening in Germany through a telescope in his bedroom. Dr. Willis had the king bound tightly so that he could not run wildly throughout the house. On Christmas Day, William learned from William Pitt that the king believed he had a newborn son, whom he named Prince Octavius. The new prince was in fact a feather pillow.

Two days later, on December 27, 1788, William received news that his aunt Hannah had died, eleven years to the day after her husband, William's uncle, had died. William organized her funeral and thought about the wonderful influence she and Uncle William had had in his life. They had opened his eyes to what real faith in God was. For a while he had turned his back on that faith, but once more he had come to embrace it. And now that faith was guiding him forward in his quest to see an end to the indignity and ungodliness of slavery.

In January 1789, William Pitt came under immense pressure to declare the Prince of Wales regent. He tried to hold off as long as he could, until he ran out of excuses and knew he had to negotiate with the prince. He told William the best he could hope for was a negotiation that limited some of the regent's power.

William Pitt's negotiation with the Prince of Wales bogged down quickly and went nowhere. Then in February 1789, two things happened that gave William Wilberforce hope for the future. The first was that King George III regained his sanity, sweeping aside the need to appoint a regent in his stead and securing Pitt's position as prime minister. The second thing was William's meeting with a man named James Stephen.

For six years James Stephen, now thirty years old, had served as a government trade lawyer on the island of St. Kitts in the Caribbean. As he sat on the leather couch in William's home at Old Palace Yard, he had a story to tell. Soon after arriving in the Caribbean in 1783, James had traveled to Barbados, where he witnessed the trial of four African slaves accused of murdering a white doctor. As he watched the trial, it became clear to him that the four men were innocent and the only witness, a fifteen-year-old slave girl, was lying out of fear of her master. Of course the four men were found guilty and sentenced to be burned at the stake for their crime. Two of the men somehow managed to avoid the ultimate punishment, but James watched as the other two slaves were killed. At that moment, James told William, he vowed never to own a slave and instead divert as much energy as he could into the effort to abolish slavery.

James went on to give William lots of information about the grim realities of the slave trade in the Caribbean. He also explained that he had come home to England for the birth of his third son, James, who was now two weeks old. He intended to return to St. Kitts soon to continue working as a lawyer. He promised William he would gather information, keep detailed records on the Caribbean slave trade, and correspond regularly.

William was grateful that he'd met James. He considered him to be an important piece of the abolition movement, since it was difficult to find reputable men who knew the slave trade as well as James did but were not part of it.

In April 1789 the Privy Council committee released to Parliament its report on the slave trade's effects on British commerce. William read every word of the 850-page report, which was filled with all manner of damning facts about the slave trade. In some of what he read, William found it hard to believe that one human being could inflict such inhumanity upon another person. Surely, he reasoned, anyone in Parliament who read the report would have no other option but to vote for the abolition of the slave trade in the British Empire.

Later that month William traveled to Barham Court in Teston, Kent, to meet with the other abolitionists. Sir Charles and Lady Margaret Middleton were there, as were James Ramsay, Thomas Clarkson, and Hannah More. They had much to talk about. William gave an overview of the grim realities described in the Privy Council committee's report. He also had with him a special poem. William had asked John Newton to persuade his friend and fellow hymn writer and poet, William Cowper, to compose a poem for the movement. The poem, titled "The Negro's Complaint," talked about how England called itself a Christian nation while enslaving and mistreating hundreds of thousands of Africans. William found the last verse particularly moving:

> Deem our nation brutes no longer,
> Till some reason ye shall find
> Worthier of regard and stronger
> Than the colour of our kind.
> Slaves of gold, whose sordid dealings
> Tarnish all your boasted powers,
> Prove that you have human feelings,
> Ere you proudly question ours!

How true it is, William thought as he read the poem aloud to the group. *England is tarnishing its reputation by continuing the slave trade.*

Thomas also brought something to the meeting that he felt served as a powerful symbol of the evils of the slave trade: a meticulously drawn diagram of the inside of a slave ship, the *Brookes*. The diagram depicted the way in which 482 human beings were packed in below deck so that the vessel could carry the maximum number of slaves. William was deeply moved as he stared at the picture, noting the tiny depictions of slaves laid out in rows like matches in a box. He was even more disturbed after Thomas pointed out that the number of slaves depicted (482) was what the ship was now allowed to carry under William Dolben's Slave Trade Act. Before that, the *Brookes* had carried as many as 740 slaves on the Middle Passage from Africa to the Caribbean. William was stunned. How could that many humans even fit below deck?

Those in attendance at Barham Court agreed that thousands of copies of the poem and the diagram of the *Brookes* should be printed for distribution. The more people who saw the real conditions slaves endured on the Middle Passage and who thought about a true Christian's role in recognizing the feelings of other human beings, the better.

William returned to London ready for the most important speech he'd ever made. At 5:00 p.m. on May 12, 1789, two years to the day since he, William Pitt, and Pitt's cousin William Grenville had rested beneath the spreading oak tree on Pitt's Holwood estate and talked about slavery, William Wilberforce stood before Parliament and launched into an impassioned speech calling for the abolition of the slave trade. William started by expressing how inadequate he felt to the task before him and then acknowledged, "I mean not to accuse any one but to take the shame upon myself, in common indeed with the whole Parliament of Great Britain, for having suffered this horrid trade to be carried on under their authority. We are all guilty."

William went on to explain in great detail the horrors of the Middle Passage, drawing on information he had gleaned from the Privy Council report, from Thomas Clarkson, and from James Stephen. This was followed by a point-by-point rebuttal of the arguments made in support of the slave trade, again drawing on actual examples of the brutality and inhumanity of slavery. In closing, William declared,

> The nature and all the circumstances of this Trade are now laid open to us. We can no longer plead ignorance, we cannot evade it, it is now an object placed before us, we cannot pass it. We may spurn it, we may kick it out of our way, but we cannot turn aside so as to avoid seeing it. For it is brought now so directly before our eyes that this House must decide, and must justify to all the world, and to their own conscience, the rectitudes of their grounds and of the principles of their decision. . . . Let not Parliament be the only body that is insensible to national justice.

With that, William bowed slightly and sat down. He had spoken for three and a half hours.

Chapter 11

Who Can Be Against You?

William Wilberforce was wrong. He had told Parliament that they could not ignore the slave trade any longer. They had heard the evidence. The eyes of the country and the world were upon them, and they would have to act. Either they voted to allow the slave trade to continue or they voted to put an end to it once and for all. Instead they chose a third way. They asked to hear more evidence before making a decision, and with that, Parliament broke for its summer recess.

This was not what William had expected, and he could hardly sleep. At night thousands of branded, beaten, starving, wretchedly ill African men, women, and children populated his dreams. He knew he had let them down. As he lay in bed, he imagined the slave ships plying the Middle Passage, taking a new batch of slaves to their doom. He found it hard to forgive his fellow members of Parliament for refusing to deal with the problem.

As he thought about the outcome in the House of Commons, William recalled the letter that Thomas Clarkson had received from John Wesley, the aging founder of the Methodists. Wesley had written,

> I desire to forewarn you that you must expect difficulties and great opposition from those who are interested in the system of slavery. They are a powerful body, and they will raise all their forces when they perceive their craft to be in danger. They will employ hired writers, who will have neither justice nor mercy. But the Committee is not to be dismayed by such treatment, nor even if some of those who professed goodwill toward you should turn against you. . . . I commend you to Him who is able to carry you through all opposition and support you under all discouragements.

At the time William had thought that Wesley was being too pessimistic. Now he understood exactly what he meant.

William returned to Barham Court to regroup with the Middletons and various other abolitionists. He had hoped to go to France and meet with opponents of the slave trade, but bigger things were brewing in France. Political unrest in the country had been going on for several years, and it looked as if the country would be falling into outright revolution.

A riot in which twenty-five protesters were killed had occurred in Paris the month before, and a convocation calling for a complete change of government in France was currently under way. None of this deterred William, but his friends pointed out that given the current political climate in France, any representative of the British government was likely to be harassed or even killed. Thomas Clarkson volunteered to go to France in William's place.

News from France continued to be alarming. On June 17, 1789, a new constituent assembly, whose representatives were drawn from commoners, declared itself to be France's new National Assembly and charged itself with creating a French constitution. At first King Louis XVI opposed the new assembly but in the end was forced to accept it. Things got quickly out of hand, however, when the king dismissed and banished his finance minister, Jacques Necker, who was sympathetic to the authority of the new assembly. Fear over this action spread throughout Paris. Rumor had it that this was the start of a pushback by the king against the new National Assembly and that troops would soon be entering Paris to reassert the monarch's authority. Three days later, on July 14, a mob stormed the Bastille, a largely disused medieval fortress and prison in the center of Paris that represented royal authority in the city. By the time the storming of the Bastille was over, ninety-eight people had been killed and the governor of the fortress and the mayor of Paris executed. There was no doubt in William's mind, or anyone else's in Great Britain, that France was in the grip of full-on revolt.

Several days after news of the storming of the Bastille reached England, William received more bad news, this time closer to home. James Ramsay, the vicar at Teston and a tireless abolitionist, had died while resting at Sir Charles Middleton's townhouse in London. His body was returned to Teston, where he was buried in the yard of the church where he had served as vicar. This was a sobering time for William and everyone else in the abolitionist movement. Although James's cause of death was unclear, it seemed likely that at fifty-five years of age he had died from the stress of opposing the slave trade. William knew that James had often worried about the threats he received on his life and about the terrible lies the proslavery forces heaped on him.

Following the funeral, William went to Cowslip Green in Somerset with his sister Sally to relax and enjoy the country air. Regrettably, that did not work out. At Cowslip Green, William and Sally stayed with Hannah and Martha More in their summer cottage. One day, Martha insisted they pack William a picnic lunch and sent him off to Cheddar Gorge. William was eager to go. He had heard of the natural beauty of this limestone gorge in the Mendip Hills and the many caves throughout the area, and he wanted to see it for himself. What William didn't anticipate was the squalid conditions under which the people of the Mendip area lived. There was no school for the children and no church to minister to the spiritual needs of the people. Some families lived in hovels, while others made their homes in the caves, and all seemed to exist at a level of subsistence William found hard to grasp. In fact, William was so shocked by what he saw that he didn't eat a thing from the picnic hamper packed for him. The sight of such destitution drained his appetite.

William returned to the More sisters' summer cottage deeply troubled. He knew he had to do something to help the bedraggled people he had seen that day. He discussed the situation with Hannah, and before the night was over they had come to an agreement. Hannah would devise a plan to establish schools for the children of the Mendip area, and William would pay for them.

As William continued to send money for the schools, he received regular letters telling him how grateful the people of the area were for his generosity. For the first time, the children of Mendip were learning to read and write and to hope for a better life. William was delighted to hear that things with the schools were going well, because things with the bill to end the slave trade were not.

When Parliament began its new session in January 1790, William put forward a motion that instead of all the members of the House of Commons being involved in further investigation of the slave trade, the matter be sent to a Select Committee. This committee would hear testimony from witnesses for and against the trade and report its findings back to the House. The motion passed, and William was appointed to the Select Committee. Soon he was spending five hours each day hearing testimony and interrogating witnesses and was using his evenings to take care of other parliamentary business. As the weeks rolled by, the pile of pages of testimony and evidence presented to the Select Committee began to grow.

As the work of the Select Committee dragged on, the proslavery lobby spent their time whipping up fear about ending the slave trade. They wrote their own pamphlets and sent spies into the abolition meetings being held around the country. William was outraged when he saw some of the pamphlets published by the anti-abolitionists. One pamphlet declared,

> It is well known that the eastern and western coasts of Africa are inhabited by stupid and unenlightened hordes; immersed in the most gross and impenetrable gloom of barbarism, dark in mind as in body, prodigiously populous, impatient of all control, unteachably lazy. . . . The traffic [shipping slaves to the plantations in the Caribbean] has proved a fortunate event for . . . [these] . . . miserable captives.

Nothing made William's blood boil more than such lies. He had to look only as far as his dining room to know they were not true. Across the table sat Olaudah Equiano, a freed slave who was one of the most well-spoken, cultured, Christian men William had met. As a boy of eleven, Equiano had been kidnapped from his village of Essaka among the Igbo people, taken to the coast, and sold into slavery. He was shipped on the Middle Passage to Barbados in the Caribbean and then sent on to the Virginia colony. Eventually he was able to buy his freedom and left North America to settle as a free man in England.

In the course of his life, Equiano had traveled by ship all over the world and had even been to the Arctic. Not only could he speak English eloquently, but also he wrote it superbly. The year before, he had written and published his own memoir titled *The Interesting Narrative of the Life of Olaudah Equiano.* In the book he gave a powerful depiction of the horrors of slavery that he and other slaves had endured. The book was so well written and interesting that it was hard to keep up with demand. Already it had been reprinted several times, and Equiano was waiting for another batch of books to arrive from the printer so he could once again get busy selling and autographing them and helping to push forward the cause of abolition. *He is one of those supposed "stupid and unenlightened hordes,"* William fumed to himself, *and he has achieved more than most enlightened Englishmen.*

Because William was a man of action, it was hard for him to sit day after day, week after week on the Select Committee, listening to witness after witness testify. He already knew without a shadow of doubt that slavery was a great moral evil, an affront to God, and the blight on the soul of Great Britain that must be stamped out as fast as possible. Instead, he was stuck hearing testimony.

During this time news arrived in England from West Africa. Three years before, the Committee for the Relief of the Black Poor had been formed in London. William was aware of the committee but did not have much to do with it, given how busy he was, trying to get Parliament to outlaw the slave trade. The "Black Poor" in the committee's name were former slaves who had fought with the British against the American colonists in the American War of Independence and had been evacuated to England when the British lost the fight. Under the auspices of the committee, run by Granville Sharp, 280 black men, 70 white women, 40 black women, and some English tradesmen had set sail from Portsmouth on April 9, 1787, bound for Sierra Leone on the west coast of Africa. Some of the group were former slaves who had been born in Africa and were "going home." Others were born in America and had never before seen Africa. Their purpose in going was to establish what was to be the Province of Freedom, a place where they could live as freemen, grow crops, and develop a thriving community.

Things didn't go well from the start. A number of the group died on the voyage. After their arrival in Sierra Leone, the survivors became involved in conflict with the local Africans of the Temne and Mende tribes, who resisted the encroachment into their territory. Nonetheless, the group persisted. They built Granville Town and cleared land and planted crops. But the harsh tropical climate often caused their crops to fail, and many people died of disease. Then, after two and a half years of struggle, a local chief attacked and destroyed Granville Town, killing many more of the group.

When William received news of the demise of Granville Town in early 1790, he was disappointed.

He'd had high hopes that the endeavor would be a success and more freed slaves would be able to join the group there. Still, he hoped it was only a temporary setback and that the Committee for the Relief of the Black Poor would continue in its efforts until the Province of Freedom was a firm and stable reality in Sierra Leone.

On September 11, 1790, William attended his sister Sally's wedding in Hull. Sally married the Reverend Thomas Clarke, the vicar of Hull's Holy Trinity Church. Thomas was a widower and one of the town's leading abolitionists. William found it hard to get used to the idea that his only living sister was now a married woman. It reminded him that at thirty-one years of age, he was still single and far too involved with ending the slave trade to think about courting a young woman.

A full year went by with no bill to end the slave trade being passed by Parliament. In January 1791, William, along with Henry Thornton, visited his friend Thomas Gisborne at Yoxall Lodge in Needwood Forest, Staffordshire. William and Thomas had known each other at Cambridge, but at that time they'd had little in common. William was busy having fun while Thomas was studying hard. However, Thomas, who occupied the room behind William's, could sometimes be lured to William's room late in the evening for a glass of sherry and a slice of Yorkshire pie. Now Thomas was a well-known preacher and country parson, and in the years since William had become a Christian, the two men had developed a firm friendship. Thomas Babington, another

Cambridge friend, was also at Yoxall Lodge. His sister Mary was married to Thomas Gisborne.

William loved visiting Yoxall, especially walking through the medieval forest that surrounded the place. But this time William had come to Yoxall Lodge to work, and Thomas Babington had agreed to help him. The two men set up an office in one of the upstairs bedrooms and set to work on the daunting task ahead of them. William had with him over ten thousand pages of testimony regarding the slave trade that had been presented to the Select Committee the previous year and that now needed to be summarized. That was the easy part. The two men would then use the collected evidence to develop arguments against the slave trade and use various pieces of the testimony and information collected to bolster those arguments.

For the next two months William and Thomas Babington barely stepped outside the house. They worked on the papers from dawn until late into the evening, pausing only for a half-hour dinner break. They were racing against the clock. In mid-April William was scheduled to speak once again in the House of Commons for a bill to end the slave trade.

As the two men worked together at Yoxall Lodge, William received a letter from John Wesley on February 24, 1791. The eighty-seven-year-old founder of Methodism wanted to encourage William in the fight against slavery.

> I see not how you can go through your glorious enterprise in opposing that execrable villainy,

> which is the scandal of religion, of England, and of human nature. Unless God has raised you up for this very thing, you will be worn out by the opposition of men and devils. But if God be for you, who can be against you? Are all of them together stronger than God? O be not weary of well doing! Go on, in the name of God and in the power of his might, till even American slavery (the vilest that ever saw the sun) shall vanish away before it. Reading this morning a tract [written] by a poor African, I was particularly struck by that circumstance that a man who has a black skin, being wronged or outraged by a white man, can have no redress; it being a "law" in our colonies that the oath of a black against a white goes for nothing. What villainy is this? That he who has guided you from youth up may continue to strengthen you in this and all things, is the prayer of, dear sir,
>
> Your affectionate servant, John Wesley.

William appreciated the encouragement, especially since he knew that Wesley was physically frail. In fact, just a few days afterward, William received a letter informing him that John Wesley had died and that his letter to William was the last one he ever wrote.

In April, William once again took to the floor of the House of Commons to give an impassioned speech in favor of a bill to end the slave trade. He summed up his arguments by saying,

> Let us not despair; it is a blessed cause, and success, ere long, will crown our exertions. Already we have gained one victory; we have obtained, for these poor creatures, the recognition of their human nature, which, for a while was most shamefully denied. This is the first fruits of our efforts; let us persevere and our triumph will be complete. Never, never will we desist till we have wiped away this scandal from the Christian name, released ourselves from the load of guilt under which we at present labour, and extinguished every trace of this bloody traffic, of which our posterity, looking back to the history of these enlightened times, will scarce believe that it has been suffered to exist so long a disgrace and dishonour to this country. Whatever may be its success, I attach my happiness to their cause and shall never relinquish it. Supported as I have been, indeed, such a desertion would be most despicable, I have already gained for the wretched Africans the recognition of their claim to the rank of human beings, and I doubt not but the Parliament of Great Britain will no longer withhold from them the rights of human nature!

Regrettably, Parliament did withhold those rights. In a vote taken on April 18, 1791, 163 members of the House of Commons voted against William's bill to end the slave trade, and 88 members voted for it. It was another defeat. William returned to his house at Old Palace Yard and reread John Wesley's letter. "Unless God has raised you up for this very thing, you will be worn out by the opposition of men and devils. But if God be for you, who can be against you? Are all of them together stronger than God?" *No,* William thought, *they are not. I have been called to this task. I cannot, I will not forget the fifty thousand people a year taken—kidnapped from Africa, tortured and assaulted on the Middle Passage, and dumped in the Caribbean where they are worked to death. With God's help I will fight on.* And fight on he did.

Following the departure of the group to Sierra Leone under the auspices of the Committee for the Relief of the Black Poor in 1787, another group of freed slaves who had evacuated to England at the end of the American War of Independence was sent to Nova Scotia to live and make a new life for themselves. Unfortunately, the climate and the continual racism they faced made their stay in Nova Scotia less than desirable. Something had to be done about the situation, and Henry Thornton presented a bill to Parliament to do just that. Despite fierce opposition to the proposal, on July 1, 1791, Parliament passed the bill establishing the Sierra Leone Company. The plan called for those black loyalists now in Nova Scotia to be sent to Sierra Leone to live. But this time they would not be establishing a Province of Freedom in which they could subsist. Instead the new venture would be set up as a trade venture. Trading posts would be established and a trade with England developed, which would help to sustain the new arrivals and benefit the local Africans.

A board of directors was established for the new company, with Henry Thornton as its chairman and William, Thomas Clarkson, Charles Grant, Thomas Babington, and Sir Charles Middleton serving as directors. William was pleased to be made a director. He was certain that the weaknesses in the previous attempt had been addressed, and he felt that the new venture would be a success. A number of entrepreneurs in Great Britain also supported the project.

With France still in political turmoil, many in England closely watched the situation, wondering how it would play out. The volatile situation spread to France's Caribbean colonies, in particular Saint-Domingue (Haiti), where in August 1791 a bloody slave revolt took place. Within a few days of the revolt breaking out, the rebelling slaves controlled most of Saint-Domingue.

News of the slave revolt was met with fear in Great Britain, and the anti-abolitionists were quick to seize on that fear. The uncertainty over the fate of slavery created by William Wilberforce and the other abolitionists could easily lead to the same thing happening in Great Britain's Caribbean colonies. What use would it be, the anti-abolitionists argued, if all the English people on the Caribbean islands were slaughtered and the slaves were left with no laws or livelihood? Better to maintain the status quo.

As a result, more personal attacks were heaped upon William, who heard stories that he was secretly married to a black slave, that he kept slaves himself, and that his money was all tied up in a slave ship.

Captain Horatio Nelson, one of the British naval heroes of the war with the American colonies, called William a hypocrite and a main cause of unrest in the Caribbean. He proudly declared, "I was bred in the good old school and taught to appreciate the value of our West Indian possessions, and neither in the field nor [in] the senate shall their just rights be infringed while I have an arm to fight in their defense or a tongue to launch my voice against the damnable doctrine of Wilberforce and his hypocritical allies." William dryly noted the self-interest behind Nelson's remarks. Nelson was married to the daughter of a leading slave-owning family on the island of Nevis in the Caribbean.

Despite the personal attacks on him, William was not about to give up the fight. He had committed himself to ending slavery in the British Empire, and he would fight to the bitter end to achieve that goal.

Chapter 12

A Better Hour Is Near

On April 2, 1792, for the third time in four years, William Wilberforce stood before the House of Commons to introduce a bill to abolish the slave trade. Some of his fellow parliamentarians joked about his bill being like a daffodil or crocus—popping up every spring, only to wither and die before summer. Still, William was determined to have his say, put the matter before Parliament, and make them vote.

The previous year had been a busy one for abolitionists. Groups supporting abolition had sprung up all over England and Scotland. Thomas Clarkson and William Dickson were sent to encourage these groups to collect signatures on petitions supporting the bill and take them back to William. As they traveled, Thomas Clarkson and William Dickson took two "weapons" with them: thousands of the oval pottery cameo brooches Josiah Wedgewood had produced, featuring the logo of the Committee for the Abolition of the Slave Trade—including the words "Am I not a man and a brother?"—and a newly printed pamphlet called *Abstract of Evidence*. The pamphlet included the diagram of the slave ship *Brookes* and a summary of the facts about the slave trade and how it affected Africa and the West Indian colonies.

The results of the petition drive astonished everyone. The mood in Great Britain had changed, and many people wanted an end to the slave trade. Most wanted an immediate end to England's involvement in slavery altogether but were persuaded to sign a petition supporting something that fell short of the total abolition of slavery. By the time the debate opened in the House of Commons in early April, rolls and rolls of petitions were ready to be unfurled on the floor of the chamber.

Charles Fox, one of the most forceful speakers in the House of Commons and a strong supporter of ending the slave trade, stood to speak first. He gave an excellent introduction to the bill. William stood and spoke next. Again he laid out his case, listing one after the other the inhumanities of the slave trade and challenging his fellow MPs that the time had come to stand with humanity and end the ghastly trade that blighted Great Britain. "Look to the continent of Africa, and there you will behold such a scene of horrors no tongue can express, no imagination can imagine," he implored as he ended his speech.

James Braille, a Scottish MP, was the first to speak for the opposition. He put the blame for the bloodshed in the French colony of Saint-Domingue on the shoulders of abolitionists. He wanted to know how Britain, with a ratio of sixteen black slaves to every white person in Jamaica, would protect its fine and loyal subjects if their slaves caught the same desire for freedom. What right did the abolitionists have to create so much havoc in one of Great Britain's colonies? Didn't words like *freedom*, *liberty*, and *reform* have a darker side? The members of the House of Commons need only look as far as France, or even to Birmingham in England itself, to see what havoc "new and subversive" ideas could bring.

William, and everyone else in Parliament, knew what Braille was talking about. Nine months before, riots had broken out in Birmingham when scientist and philosopher Joseph Priestley organized a dinner to celebrate the second anniversary of the storming of the Bastille in Paris. People took to the streets, attacking those attending the dinner and then burning Dr. Priestley's beautiful home and laboratory, along with several dissenter churches in the city, to the ground. Three days of rioting followed in which twenty-six other homes and three more churches were burned. Joseph Priestley would have most likely been killed had he not managed to escape to London. It was common knowledge afterward that the Birmingham magistrates had planned the attack on Dr. Priestley and provided the weapons to carry it out. Even King George III, who eventually sent troops to quell the violence, announced, "I feel pleased that Priestley is the sufferer for the doctrines he and his party have instilled, and that the people see them in their true light."

James Braille passionately brought his speech to a close by outlining the terrible consequences involved in ending the slave trade: several hundred ships and their crews, along with millions of dockworkers, shipbuilders, and factory workers, would be instantly out of jobs. So what good was any kind of reform of the slave trade if it created widespread poverty at home?

When Braille sat down, Henry Dundas rose to speak. He was another Scottish MP who was also home secretary and William Pitt's right-hand man. He was powerful in all ways: tall and well built and known as "King Harry the Ninth" for his influence over Scottish politics. William was not sure what Dundas was going to say but thought that because of his ties to William Pitt he would not speak in favor of the slave trade and therefore against the prime minister. The great Scottish MP spoke slowly and deliberately. "I have long held the same opinion of the slave trade as my friends MP Wilberforce and Prime Minister Pitt. Where we differ is in how we would bring its end about."

William glanced up at the gallery. He spotted Olaudah Equiano staring down intently at the proceedings.

"I stand against the slave trade," William heard Dundas continue in his booming voice, "but not for its immediate and abrupt abolition. I propose a middle road, a moderate road—the gradual ending of the slave trade. I rise to move an amendment to the bill, which is to insert the word *gradually* before the words *to be abolished*. The motion then will be that the slave trade ought gradually to be abolished."

William's heart sank. He knew it was over. Even though William Pitt followed with one of the best speeches he'd ever given, the damage was done. Dundas had given those MPs who sat on the fence, those who did not want to vote one way or the other, an escape route. They could stay on the fence and vote yes and look as though they were acting in a concerned and thoughtful way, knowing that their vote would not take effect until some time in the future, if ever. When the date for the abolition of the slave trade was set as January 1, 1796, the bill, with the word *gradually* inserted, passed the House of Commons by a vote of 230 to 85.

Following the vote, many people congratulated William. Finally a bill to end the slave trade had passed! Even John Newton's friend, the famous poet William Cowper, wrote a poem to celebrate and honor William:

> Thou has achiev'd a part, hast gain'd the ear
> Of Britain's senate to thy glorious cause;
> Hope smiles, joy springs and tho' cold caution pause,
> And weave delay, the better hour is near.

The bill entered the House of Lords for approval on May 3, 1792. In the House of Commons it had passed overwhelmingly, and the names of 390,000 British citizens registered on petitions in favor of ending the slave trade had also been presented, yet the members of the House of Lords refused to be impressed. The king's third son, William, the Duke of Clarence, insisted that he had proof that the evidence presented to the House of Commons had been wrong and that the black slaves were all well treated in Jamaica. Further, he argued, if the members of the House of Lords were merely there to agree with everything that the House of Commons sent to them, they would be a useless body and soon have nothing to do. Such a bill as this might bring down British society completely, and the Duke of Clarence asked that the bill be stopped until further investigation into the real state of the slave trade was carried out.

"Haven't we investigated enough?" William snapped on hearing the news. He thought of the Privy Council inquiry and report and all the evidence that had been presented to the Select Committee and the House of Commons. It was obvious the members of the House of Lords were looking for a way to stall the bill when they agreed with the Duke of Clarence that more evidence was needed. The bill was tucked away, and no one seemed to be able to find time to start a new round of investigations.

Even though William had half expected this outcome, it was still a bitter defeat. How would he ever get the House of Lords to vote for something when they had so much to lose? He didn't know. All he knew was that he had to keep trying. He found it hard to believe, as the line from William Cowper's poem suggested, that "the better hour is near."

Two weeks later, on a beautiful spring morning in May, William found himself walking on the west side of Clapham Common with his cousin and best friend Henry Thornton. Accompanying them was Charles

Grant. Two years earlier Charles had returned from twenty-three years as a government administrator in India. As the men walked, Charles spoke in his strong Scottish accent. "Now, I can see with my own eyes what you're talking about, Henry. What a bonnie spot this is. Think what we could do if we were all neighbors. What do ye think, William?"

William walked on in silence. He had a lot to think about. Henry's deceased father, John Thornton, had lived with his family on the south side of the Common, and his sons Samuel and Robert (Henry's brothers) also lived there. Henry, who had grown rich from his banking and manufacturing interests, had bought Battersea Rise, a beautiful Queen Anne mansion on the west side of the Common. His plan, if Charles agreed, was to subdivide his large property so that Edward Eliot and Charles could each build his own home there as well. Then William, who did not need his own large house, would move in with Henry, who was also still single. The two men would live together, sharing expenses in a "chummery" surrounded by the Thornton brothers, Charles Grant and his family, and Edward Eliot, along with his motherless daughter, Harriot.

"Not only would we all be neighbors, but John Venn has agreed to become our parish clergyman." Charles's eyes shone as he spoke.

"Wonderful," William agreed. He'd heard the Reverend Venn speak several times and admired his strong, thoughtful sermons.

"Can you imagine the fellowship we would enjoy, the facility to do good?" Henry added. "With Granville

Sharp already living in Clapham village, and my brothers, then the two of you and Edward—we could attend to Sierra Leone Company matters as soon as they arose."

"We'll need to support each other and each other's families," William agreed. "The anti-abolitionists are becoming more vicious each day." He walked on, recalling a poem he'd been given a copy of when leaving Parliament the day before. It was by James Boswell, a man who started out standing with the abolitionists and now, by the scathing tone and content of his poem, clearly did not.

Go Wilberforce, with narrow skull,
Go home and preach away at Hull.
No longer to the Senate cackle
In strains that suit the tabernacle;
I hate your little whittling sneer,
Your pert and self-sufficient leer.
Mischief to trade sits on your lip.
Insects will gnaw the noblest ship.
Go, Wilberforce, begone, for shame,
Thou dwarf with big resounding name.

Yes, William thought as he recalled the poem, *perhaps it is God's will for us to live in community here in Clapham and support each other.* The town was just five miles from Westminster and Parliament. Although it was not as far out in the country as William would have liked, it did have a village atmosphere. William decided he could relax here, and he surely needed that. Since presenting the latest bill to abolish the slave trade, not one but two slave ship captains were harassing him over testimony given during debate on the bill. William had questioned the first man, Captain Rolleston, during the debate, and members of Parliament had laughed at some of the captain's muddled answers. In turn, the captain had challenged William to a duel, stating that only one man was worthy of living. William refused. He hated the idea of dueling, seeing it as an upper-class form of murder.

The second man, Captain Kimber, had been exposed in Parliament for flogging a fifteen-year-old slave girl to death on the deck of his ship. He had been tried for the incident and declared innocent. Still the facts remained, and William used them and the captain's name in his argument about the cruelty of the Middle Passage. As a result, Captain Kimber was demanding from William a public apology, five thousand pounds, and a good government position. When William refused the demand, Captain Kimber began stalking him, following him home at night, and harassing him on the street. William's friends urged him to carry a gun and hire a bodyguard. Reluctantly he did both, but he tried not to worry, telling himself that either way things would turn out fine. If the captain managed to kill him, his death might well do more good for the cause of abolition than if he were alive.

William moved into Battersea Rise, Henry Thornton's elegant home, and soon two new houses were taking shape beside it. Charles Grant called his new home Glenelg, after his parish in Scotland, and

Edward Eliot decided to call his Broomfield Lodge. The men joined forces at Clapham Common just in time. The year 1792 was a pivotal year in England, and William was glad to have his closest friends within walking distance.

In Paris on August 10, 1792, French Republican forces stormed the royal Tuileries Palace. More than eight hundred Swiss guardsmen and other royalist defenders were killed before King Louis XVI and his family were captured and imprisoned. The downfall of the French monarchy sent shock waves through the British aristocracy. France's old order had been swept aside in favor of a new government of the people.

While the British aristocracy was alarmed, there were those in England who sympathized somewhat with the French Republicans. One such group was the London Corresponding Society, founded in January 1792 by a lawyer named John Frost and Thomas Hardy, a shoemaker. The aim of the group was to bring parliamentary reform to Great Britain, giving the people, especially the working class, more representation and a greater say in the affairs of the country. Many of William's friends, including Olaudah Equiano, had joined the group, though William was aware that many viewed the London Corresponding Society with suspicion.

Things grew tense on both sides of the English Channel until January 21, 1793, when the government of the new Republic of France executed King Louis XVI at the guillotine. When William heard the news, he mused at how fickle things could be: the king who had done so much to help the Americans in their Revolutionary War had himself been killed by revolutionaries in his own country. The following month France declared war on Great Britain.

Because the House of Lords had done nothing with the bill to bring about a gradual abolition of the slave trade, William once again entered into the House of Commons his old bill for total abolition of the trade. The bill went nowhere. The beheading of the king of France had created a chill among the British aristocracy. Lords and dukes squashed anything that hinted at liberty, or democracy, or human rights. William knew that his bill did not have a chance of passing in such an atmosphere, and he was right. The bill was soundly defeated in Parliament. The Duke of Clarence even stated that "the promoters of abolition are either fanatics or hypocrites." William was devastated. The real chance for change had been the previous year, and now it was too late.

William was aware that many people now expected him to step back from the fight. After all, for the past five years, he had tried to get his bill to end the slave trade through Parliament, and now achieving that goal seemed farther away than ever. Nonetheless, in February 1794, William was back in the House of Commons arguing for yet another anti-slave-trading bill. Another failure followed.

By now many of William's supporters had grown weary and discouraged. Ending the slave trade seemed like an impossible dream, and William had to admit that if he did not believe that God had called him to the task, he would have given up too.

One man who did step aside at this point was Thomas Clarkson. Thomas had been a tireless researcher for the abolitionist movement. In his fourteen years of involvement in the cause, he had traveled over thirty-five thousand miles, survived death threats, endured insults and attacks on his character, and collected thousands of pages of evidence on the evils of slavery. By now, he admitted to William, he was physically and emotionally worn out. Nothing could make him get back on a horse and take up the cause. He just could not do it. William understood. It was hard, very hard, to keep going, and Thomas had borne the brunt of many attacks. Now, seven years after William stood under the spreading oak tree with William Pitt and William Grenville at Pitt's Holwood estate, much had changed. Two of the abolitionists' most tireless workers, James Ramsay and Thomas Clarkson—one dead, one exhausted—were gone, and the goal seemed farther away than when they had started.

Chapter 13

Great Contentment

Thank God I have Clapham! William told himself. It was the one place where he could both relax and work. By spring 1796 he'd been living for four years at Battersea Rise with Henry Thornton. During that time two wings were added to the house, bringing the total number of bedrooms to thirty-four. William Pitt, who often came to stay, was drawing up plans for a magnificent oval addition to the house that would be used as a library and meeting room. Those who lived around Clapham Common certainly needed a central place to meet among themselves and with guests about the various ways to bring about the "moral improvement" of England.

Each man and woman in the group brought his or her own set of interests to the attention of the others. As a result William found himself caught up in more causes than he thought possible. Charles Grant was convinced that the East India Company should not act like rulers in India, keeping missionaries and teachers out. That year, he wrote a tract entitled *Observations on the State of Society among the Asiatic Subjects of Great Britain.*

William did what he could to help Charles get his message out. In many ways he saw India as he did Africa: British citizens sailed to foreign shores and created havoc for the indigenous people. The local people's rights were never thought about back in Great Britain. No one seemed to care how the kidnapping of millions of Africans or the upsetting of the balance of power between the Indian princes impacted their societies. William hoped that Charles's tract would bring this to the attention of the British people.

Hannah More and her sisters were frequent guests at Battersea Rise, and everyone took an interest in Hannah's schools. When Hannah decided to write moral stories and publish them cheaply so that almost anyone could afford them, Henry Thornton offered to be her business partner. He even tried his hand at writing a few tracts himself.

On March 1, 1796, everything changed for William. Henry, a confirmed bachelor, suddenly married. His bride was none other than William's childhood friend from Hull, Marianne Sykes.

After the wedding William continued to live at Battersea Rise, but when he learned that Marianne was expecting a baby, he returned to his house at 4 Old Palace Yard. There was a lot to keep him busy there. He worked with Sir Thomas Bernard on a new scheme, a Society for Bettering the Condition and Increasing the Comforts of the Poor. He also sat on a secret parliamentary committee to examine the accounts of the Bank of England.

William also started writing a book on the practice of religion. The book's title said it all: *A Practical View of the Prevailing Religious System of Professed Christians, in the Higher and Middle Classes in This Country, Contrasted with Real Christianity.* The volume attempted to point out that Christianity had become so institutionalized in Great Britain that people tended to overlook it. People believed they were Christian simply because they were born in a Christian country. In contrast, William explained what real, vibrant Christianity was like, the kind of Christianity that made a difference in people's lives on a daily basis.

On March 10, 1797, as William was finishing writing his book, Marianne Thornton gave birth to a daughter, whom she and Henry named Marianne. William was pleased for his friends, but he could not imagine himself as a married man with children. He wrote in his diary, "I doubt if I shall ever change my situation. The state of public affairs concurs with the other causes in making me believe I must finish my journey alone."

In April 1797, five hundred copies of William's book were published. Following the release of the book, William set out for Bath, where he liked to take the water treatment. His health remained frail, especially his stomach and digestive system, which proved painful at times. When he could stand the pain no longer, he would go to bed and take the laudanum the doctor prescribed for him. But William was always careful to stop taking the substance as soon as the pain diminished to a level he could endure. Laudanum, which contained opium, was addictive, and William was determined not to become addicted to it. His eyesight also continued to deteriorate. Still, William often reminded himself, he had outlived his doctor's prediction of an early death. This was good, because he still had so much he wanted to accomplish to make Great Britain a more moral and humane place.

Two days after arriving in Bath, William sat in a teahouse with his brother-in-law, Thomas Clarke, along with Thomas Babington and a group of abolitionist friends. Among them was someone he hadn't met before, a person Thomas Babington told him he should take particular notice of. Her name was Barbara Spooner. It wasn't hard to see why Thomas had singled her out: Barbara had pretty auburn curls and brown eyes. William tried to strike up a conversation with her but suddenly became tongue-tied. After lunch he questioned Thomas further about Barbara.

"Miss Spooner is twenty-five years old, the oldest daughter of Isaac Spooner, a prosperous Birmingham merchant and ironmaster. Her uncle is Henry Gough, Baron Calthorpe," Thomas informed William.

"I know Baron Calthorpe well. He's the MP for Bramber," William said.

"That's right. Miss Spooner is well connected, and what is better, she is a strong Christian. I believe she reads her Bible and prays like a Methodist."

"I must say I am very pleased with Miss Spooner," William replied. "Even though I did not converse with her much myself, I noticed that she conducted herself well with others."

Thomas smiled. "You will get to know her well. I'm sure of that. In fact, I predict you will marry her! She'll make you a wonderful wife."

The next day, Easter Sunday, William went to church, but he could not concentrate on the sermon. All he could think about was Barbara and whether, in fact, she would make him a good wife. The thought was startling, but he liked it. William decided to find reasons to spend more time with Barbara and her family. He quickly came to admire Barbara's cheerfulness and the way she respected her parents. The two of them were seen together talking at the Pump Room in Bath, and soon gossip spread about their relationship. William knew that his next move would set more tongues wagging.

The following Sunday, after a long and restless night, William wrote a letter to Barbara, asking for her hand in marriage. Within hours a reply was delivered: yes, she would marry him. William became worried. He'd known Barbara for barely a week, and now they were getting married! What had he been thinking? But as soon as he visited Barbara the next day, his doubts fled. He was sure she would be a good wife.

On Saturday, April 29, 1797, William had to pull himself away from Barbara and return to London. William Pitt had sent him an urgent letter requesting his presence in Parliament to vote on a measure for Great Britain to make a loan to Austria as the country struggled to hold off a French military advance. Back in London, William cast his vote in favor of the loan to Austria, and the measure easily passed the House of Commons. But the gesture made little difference. Before the loan could be made, news arrived in London in early May that the Austrians were negotiating a peace treaty with the French invaders.

While back at Parliament, William introduced yet another bill to abolish the slave trade, but it was quickly voted down. Great Britain was at war with France, and Napoleon and his French army were sweeping across Europe. In the present climate, few MPs were willing to risk aligning themselves with anything that would weaken the British economy or hint at giving power to the people.

With another defeat to his credit, William returned to Bath, and his wedding. William Wilberforce and Barbara Spooner were married on May 30, 1797, at St. Swithin's Church in Bath. Following the wedding, the couple traveled to the Mendip area south of Bristol for their honeymoon. They stayed in Hannah More's country cottage at Cowslip Green. While there, William showed his new bride not only the magnificent Cheddar Gorge but also the schools that Hannah had set up throughout the area to educate poor children. William still covered the cost of these schools, and he was impressed by how well they were doing. Children could now read and write, and the despair that had once hung over the place seemed to have lifted.

When William and Barbara returned to London after their honeymoon, they went to Clapham Common to stay at Broomfield Lodge, Edward Eliot's home. Edward, who was not well, and his daughter had left for the summer to stay with his parents.

A few weeks later, the Wilberforces were off again, this time to Hull to introduce Barbara to William's mother and his sister Sally. But before they arrived, a messenger intercepted them en route with news that Sally's husband, Thomas Clarke, had died suddenly. Now the newlyweds had a funeral to attend in Hull. William did his best to comfort his sister and mother after he arrived.

Back in Hull, William was shocked to find his mother openly talking about the Methodist view of Christianity. As she had aged, her ideas had changed, and she no longer looked on William's religion with contempt. William took this as a good sign and asked his old friend Joseph Milner to visit his mother and encourage her in her search for a deeper level of faith. William was delighted when he learned that Joseph had been appointed the next vicar at Hull's Holy Trinity Church. This would make Joseph's visits to his mother much easier.

After leaving Hull in September, William and Barbara returned to Bath. They had just settled in when William received news of another death. This time it was his old friend Edward Eliot. William was devastated by the news, and more so when he thought of Edward's only child, eleven-year-old Harriot, who was now an orphan. Two months later William learned that Joseph Milner also had died. He would miss his old schoolmaster and friend.

As the year drew to a close, Barbara confided in William that she was pregnant. Looking back on 1797, William could hardly believe what a year of ups and downs it had been. His book had been a runaway success, being reprinted five times and selling seventy-five hundred copies. He had started out the year a single man and was now married, with his wife expecting a child. Thankfully, the Wilberforces had a new home. William had bought Broomfield Lodge from Edward Eliot's estate.

Other families had moved into the houses that skirted Clapham Common. One of them was James Stephen, the trade lawyer who had provided William so much information about the grim realities of the slave trade in the Caribbean. That seemed so long ago now, when William was first preparing his parliamentary bill to end the slave trade. Much had changed in James's life in the intervening nine years. He was newly widowed and the father of six small children, and he had returned from St. Kitts for good. He told William he would do whatever he could to help to end the slave trade.

William's first crisis of the new year had nothing to do with the slave trade. It was about a duel. On May 28, 1798, word reached William that William Pitt had been involved in a duel the day before at Putney Heath with George Tierney, an MP representing Southwark. The two had clashed in a debate in the House of Commons, and George Tierney had challenged Pitt to the duel after he felt that the prime minister had insulted him.

Although each man fired his pistol twice during the duel, neither was injured. But the news made William angry, angrier than he had ever before been with William Pitt. Not only did William hate dueling, but also he thought the practice barbaric, a kind of sanctioned upper-class murder that went against the laws of God. To make matters worse, the duel had been held on a Sunday. William found it hard to understand how his old friend, as prime minister of Great Britain, could even agree to such a thing as taking up a gun to defend his honor. William felt he had to do something about the situation and decided to introduce a bill to Parliament outlawing dueling in Britain. The nation needed to know that such behavior would no longer be tolerated.

When William Pitt learned what William planned to do, a rift had torn open their friendship. Pitt felt that such a bill could discredit him, even end his political career, and he wrote a long letter to William explaining how he felt. After reading the letter and pondering it, William decided not to proceed with his anti-dueling bill. His intention was never to slight William Pitt or cause him political harm. In the end the two friends made up and put the incident behind them, though William wanted to believe that the prime minister would think twice before agreeing to a duel again.

With the dueling incident over, William looked forward to the birth of his first child in July. Marianne Thornton was expecting her second baby around the same time, and he hoped the two children would grow up together. Just two weeks before William and Barbara's baby was due, William received a letter from Sally informing him that their mother had died. William raced to Hull for her funeral and then back to Broomfield Lodge to be with Barbara.

William arrived back in time safely, and on Saturday, July 21, 1798, William Wilberforce Jr. was born. He was small but healthy, and William thanked God that both mother and child were doing well. Two weeks later, at Battersea Rise, Marianne gave birth to a daughter, but the baby was feeble and died within the day. William comforted Henry and Marianne as best he could. It was hard being the father of a new and healthy baby while his friends grieved the loss of their newborn child.

Time marched on. William Jr. brought delight to William and Barbara, and William found great contentment in being a father.

Meanwhile, William worked on plans to bring Zachary Macaulay, the governor of Sierra Leone for the Sierra Leone Company, back to England. The two men had met previously and become good friends. Now Zachary planned to return to England for good, bringing with him twenty-four African orphans to be educated in England. They all arrived in Clapham in May 1799. The children were housed a mile and a half away from William's house, and William often walked there to visit them.

Zachary's report to the directors of the Sierra Leone Company, including William, explained how Freetown, built on the site of the old Granville Town, had survived partial destruction and pillage at the hands of the French during 1794. The settlers had rebuilt the town, which now consisted of about four hundred buildings and a population of around twelve hundred residents. Most of the buildings in town were built in a style similar to the houses in

Nova Scotia, where many of the free slaves had lived before coming to Sierra Leone. Freetown had also developed into a bustling trading port, with ships coming and going. And a growing trade had developed with local African tribes in the interior. All in all, things seemed to be going well with the Sierra Leone Company's project in Africa. William planned to use Zachary's firsthand accounts of life in Africa in his next attempt to get Parliament to pass an anti-slave-trade bill.

By now Barbara was expecting another baby, as was Marianne Thornton. Barbara gave birth to a daughter, who was named Barbara after her, and Marianne delivered a son, who was named Henry after his father.

The year 1799 had been another busy year for William, and as January 1, 1800, approached, a fellow member of Parliament quipped to William, "Perhaps this will be the century you finally get your slave bill passed." William prayed to God that it would be.

Chapter 14

A Changing Mood

William wrote in his journal, "O Lord . . . warm my heart with love for thee, animate my sluggish nature . . . that I may not be weary in well-doing." As he put down his pen, he realized just how tired he was. It was September 1800, and he was on holiday at Bognor Rocks on the Sussex coast with Barbara, who was again pregnant, and their two children, William Jr. and Barbara, along with Henry and Marianne and their children. William had spent much of the year meeting with sugar plantation owners from the Caribbean. As a result of the war with France, the price of sugar had dropped dramatically and now fetched only half as much money at market as it had several years before.

In an effort to stabilize the falling sugar price, the plantation owners were open to suspending the slave trade for five years. The owners believed that temporarily stopping the flow of slaves into the Caribbean islands would create a labor shortage, which would slow the speed at which land could be put into sugar production. They hoped that this would stop more sugar from entering the market and in turn stabilize the price. Although the ban on the slave trade was for just five years, William saw it as the thin edge of the wedge. With no more slaves being imported into the Caribbean, plantation owners would need to take better care of the slaves they had, because if they worked them to death, there would be no replacements.

William had been hopeful at first. As part of the negotiation, he had agreed not to put forward an anti-slave-trading bill in the spring. But now it was fall, and his hopes were in tatters. The plantation owners got cold feet about the idea and could not agree upon a suitable arrangement. Nothing had changed, and the slave trade went on unhindered.

In May 1800, William's sister Sally had married James Stephen. It was the second marriage for both of them. James had six children who missed their mother, and Sally, who had no children of her own, would be taking care of them. William was concerned about his sister. Being the stepmother to six children was a challenge, and he wasn't sure how well she would cope. Despite the challenge, Sally had been determined to marry James, and now all William could do was to pray that things worked out.

The Wilberforces and the Thorntons had been vacationing at Bognor Rocks only a few days when

Barbara became ill with typhoid fever. It was a deadly disease, and William began to fret over his wife's condition. The Thorntons stepped in and took charge. Henry and Marianne arranged for all the children to be sent back to Clapham, and they called for a doctor from Bath to come and tend to Barbara. They also sent messages to Isaac Milner and James and Sally Stephen, asking them to come to Bognor Rocks.

As Barbara's condition grew steadily worse, William confided in his journal,

> It has pleased God to visit my dearest wife with a very dangerous fever. The final issue [whether she lives or dies] is not likely to be soon determined; but from the violence of the symptoms and especially the lightheadedness at the moment, I am frankly told that I have cause for the utmost apprehension, though not for despair. The thought that my dearest love has made her peace with God is an unspeakable consolation, but for this my own heart would almost sink within me.

Thankfully Barbara did not die of typhoid, though her full recovery from the disease was long and slow. On January 19, 1801, Barbara gave birth to a small, sickly daughter, whom they named Elizabeth, after William's mother. Everyone at Clapham prayed that the baby would live, especially since Barbara had become so nervous and anxious since her illness. William had noticed the change in his wife following the typhoid, and he tried to be more kind and patient with her than ever.

While William tried to spend as much time as he could at Broomfield Lodge in Clapham, there was turmoil in Parliament. On February 16, 1801, William Pitt resigned as prime minister. During 1800, the Acts of Union had been passed, one act through the British Parliament and the other through the Irish Parliament. The acts went into force on January 1, 1801, creating the new United Kingdom of Great Britain and Ireland and abolishing the Parliament of Ireland in Dublin. Instead, one hundred Irish representatives would be added to the House of Commons along with twenty-eight Irish noblemen, known as peers, and four bishops to the House of Lords.

In the abolished Irish Parliament, as in the British Parliament at Westminster, only Anglicans could be elected members. However, Ireland was a predominantly Catholic country. To entice the Irish to support the Acts of Union, William Pitt had promised what was called Catholic emancipation, allowing Roman Catholics to become members of Parliament. Although the Acts of Union did not contain language specifically setting out Catholic emancipation, it was understood that this would be part of the process of creating the new United Kingdom of Great Britain and Ireland. But when King George III refused to grant the promised Catholic emancipation, saying it violated his coronation oath as the spiritual leader of the Church of England, Pitt felt he had no option but to resign as prime minister.

William, who supported Catholic emancipation, was disappointed in the king. He wished that Pitt could have stayed on as prime minister, but he understood that because of the actions of the monarch, being unable to deliver to the Irish Catholics what had been promised them undercut Pitt's power, and so Pitt had to step down.

The king asked Henry Addington, Speaker of the House of Commons, to take Pitt's place as prime minister and form a new government. At the time Great Britain was in a weakened state. The country had been at war with France since 1793, and the ongoing cost of that war was taking a toll on the British economy, especially because the French navy had many of the ports of Europe blockaded in an effort to disrupt British trade. To help pay for the war, the new prime minister was forced to raise taxes. At the same time he entered into peace negotiations with France, and on March 25, 1802, a treaty was signed in the French city of Amiens, ending the war between Britain and France.

Although William supported Addington in his plan to make peace with the French, he felt the Treaty of Amiens was weak, especially since it did not even address the issue of abolition. This was important to William. Following the overthrow of the French monarchy and the eventual establishment of a new republican government, slaves throughout France's colonies were declared freemen. But now, under the leadership of Napoleon, France was trying to reintroduce slavery into its Caribbean colonies. As a result, William wanted the treaty to state clearly that the French would not reintroduce slavery into their colonies. William made his feelings on the matter clear to Addington, but the prime minister did not listen.

In May 1803, a group of Church of England clergymen, various Methodists, and some Baptist pastors descended on Broomfield Lodge to meet with William. During the meeting, the group's leader, the Reverend Thomas Charles, a Welsh preacher, told William about the schools he was running in Bala, Wales. One of the difficulties he faced was securing enough Bibles in Welsh for his students. He told the story of Mary Jones, a sixteen-year-old girl who had shown up at his door in Bala three years before. Mary explained that she had been saving money for six years and had walked twenty-six miles from her home to Bala to buy a copy of a Welsh Bible. Thomas's home was the closest place she could go for a copy of the Bible. Mary's determination had inspired Thomas, who, with a group of colleagues, was now in the process of setting up an organization to make copies of Welsh Bibles easily available for everyone who wanted one to read.

William was delighted as the men explained their plans to begin printing Bibles in Welsh. He suggested ways in which the group could win the favor of Church of England bishops for their project. He even offered to sit on the board of the new organization, which was to be called the British and Foreign Bible Society. Once they had printed the Bibles in Welsh, the organization would tackle Bibles in the next language, and another language after that. As one of the local Baptist pastors put it, "If for Wales, why not for the United Kingdom? Why not for the whole world?" That was the kind of thinking William Wilberforce could get behind!

May 1803 was the month war once again broke out between Britain and France, ending a yearlong peace brought about by the Treaty of Amiens. It was also the month William introduced another anti-slave-trade bill to Parliament. On May 30 the House of Commons passed the bill by a vote of 124 votes for and 49 against. The new Irish members of Parliament had helped to sway the outcome. After fourteen years, an anti-slave-trade bill without the word *gradual* grafted on it had passed its first hurdle on the way to becoming the law of the land. Now it was on to the House of Lords for final passage. Or so it should have been, until William was informed that the House of Lords had delayed voting on the bill for another year, as it was too late in the parliamentary session to thoroughly review it. The blow was crushing. Another opportunity had slipped through the abolitionists' hands.

Following the defeat, William took Barbara and their four children to Lyme Regis to recover and regroup for the summer. Elizabeth, the frail child who most people expected to die, had survived and was flourishing, and on December 19, 1802, Barbara had given birth to Robert Isaac Wilberforce. As he settled in at Lyme Regis, William reminded himself that as surely as the daffodils bloomed in spring, he would be back before Parliament next year with another anti-slave-trade bill. He was certain the House of Lords had no intention of reviewing the recently passed bill when they sat in their next session.

May 10, 1804, saw another major change in the British government. It was the day King George III reappointed William Pitt as prime minister. William was glad to see his old friend back in the political role he had been groomed for since a child. Addington's leadership as prime minister, especially his handling of the war with France, had proved ineffectual. William Pitt got right to work trying to improve things with the war effort. He forged a coalition that aligned Austria, Russia, and Sweden with Great Britain to fight against Napoleon and his army as he took control of more and more of Continental Europe.

With William Pitt back as prime minister and new Irish members in the House of Commons, William sensed that the mood of Parliament was slowly changing in favor of abolition. He began to feel it was time to gear up for one more concerted effort to abolish the slave trade. To do this he needed the best help he could find, so William wrote to Thomas Clarkson and asked him to return to active involvement in the abolitionist movement.

Thomas responded to William's letter by riding his horse to Broomfield Lodge for a meeting. William was impressed. Thomas had lost none of his old enthusiasm or vigor. After a ten-year absence from the cause, he assured William that he was ready to gear up for another round against the proslavery powers.

William was buoyed with enthusiasm as other members of the old team came to the fore again. Some were missed, however, such as Olaudah Equiano, who had died seven years before in London, though his book still sold well. William missed Equiano's strong voice in the current call to end the slave trade. But while there had been losses to the abolitionist movement, there were also gains. Henry Brougham, a brilliant young lawyer and writer from Scotland joined the antislavery "cabinet," as did another equally brilliant young aristocrat named Lord Henry Petty.

Sir Charles Middleton, who had been instrumental in bringing the abolitionist group together in the first place, was now eighty years old. Though he was unable to be as active in the organization as he had been, he gave his moral support. This was not because of his age but because William Pitt had appointed him First Lord of the Admiralty.

As a former admiral, Sir Charles had an instinctive understanding of naval logistics and strategy and was able to make quick decisions and relay them to the various admirals and captains. Sir Charles's skill as a naval leader was needed as the British navy faced off against the French and Spanish navies. What Great Britain really needed was some good news from the war with France. William hoped and prayed that as First Lord of the Admiralty, Sir Charles could help provide that, especially since things were not going well on land. Napoleon's army was bearing down on Russia and Austria, two of Great Britain's allies on the European continent.

Meanwhile, on September 7, 1805, William got his own good news. Barbara gave birth that day to another son, whom they named Samuel.

As William had hoped, good news from the war did finally arrive. Sir Charles Middleton, as First Lord of the Admiralty, had a hand in the war news. In early November, reports reached England of a crushing British naval victory against a combined French and Spanish navy. The battle had been fought on October 21, 1805, off the southwest coast of Spain, just west of Cape Trafalgar. Twenty-seven British naval ships under the leadership of Admiral Horatio Nelson aboard HMS *Victory* had engaged and defeated thirty-three French and Spanish naval ships, sinking twenty-two of the enemy vessels without the loss of a single British warship. It was a proud day for Great Britain, the kind of moment William knew the country needed. The British navy reigned supreme on the water. But the victory was tempered by loss. The hero of the day, Admiral Nelson, had been killed in the battle.

Although the British navy reigned supreme on the ocean, on land the coalition that William Pitt had forged between Great Britain, Austria, Russia, and Sweden collapsed when Napoleon's troops defeated it in the Battle of Ulm in October 1805 and the Battle of Austerlitz in December.

Great Britain was still coming to terms with the collapse of the coalition, while continuing to celebrate the victory at Trafalgar and mourn the death of Horatio Nelson, when another national event occurred. This time it was the death of Prime Minister William Pitt, who died in his London home on January 23, 1806. No one was more shocked than William Wilberforce. From the time they had met,

William had known that William Pitt drank port wine heavily in the evenings, as ordered by his doctor at age fourteen. At age forty-six, the alcohol intake had seemed to have caught up with him, and he died of liver failure.

As William stood beside the prime minister's grave at Westminster Abbey, he found it hard to believe that his old friend was gone. He thought back on the wonderful times they'd had together as twenty-year-olds. He recalled the times they'd sat side by side in the Stranger's Gallery, when William Pitt, son of Lord Chatham, one of the most revered English politicians, had explained the proceedings taking place below in the House of Commons. He thought of the wonderful holidays they'd spent together and the conversations and entertainment they'd enjoyed at Lauriston House in the Wimbledon countryside. Now it was over. The bill to end the slave trade that both Williams had tried to pass through Parliament for the past seventeen years was as elusive as ever. Before he left the graveside, William prayed a silent prayer that he would live long enough to see the bill through to the end.

Chapter 15

"The Tide Has Turned"

In all, William Pitt had been prime minister of Great Britain for twenty of the previous twenty-three years. With him gone, Parliament took on a new shape. William Pitt's cousin, William Grenville, became the new prime minister. When William Wilberforce heard the news, he sent up a silent prayer of thanks. Nineteen years before, William Grenville and William Pitt had stood with William Wilberforce beneath the spreading oak tree at Holwood and encouraged him to take up the fight to end slavery in the British Empire. Both Grenville and Pitt had pledged to do whatever they could to help Wilberforce. As well, the new prime minister had forged a political alliance with Charles Fox and his supporters. Grenville and Fox essentially were joint leaders, with Grenville serving as first lord of the treasury and Fox serving as secretary of state for foreign affairs. Fox openly supported abolition, and William felt new energy rising in Parliament toward ending the slave trade.

Soon Thomas Clarkson was once again traveling the country on horseback to speak at abolitionist meetings and stir up support for an end to the slave trade. Charles Fox convinced the Prince of Wales to agree not to interfere with any abolition bill that might make it as far as the House of Lords.

Just two months after the death of William Pitt, a bill was introduced to Parliament that attacked the slave trade in an interesting way. It had been William's brother-in-law, James Stephen, with his background in trade law, who had come up with the idea. Since Napoleon was trying to reintroduce slavery into the French colonies, James had suggested a bill that attacked the slave trade as a way to undermine French ambitions in the Caribbean. Such a bill could be presented to Parliament as a war measure. The Foreign Slave Trade Abolition Bill was thus drawn up and presented as a government measure in the House of Commons by Attorney General Sir Arthur Leary Piggott. The bill would prevent the import of slaves by British traders into territories belonging to foreign powers. While it did not outlaw the slave trade in British colonies, the bill would undermine the bulk of the British trade, since it was British slave traders who transported most of the slaves around the world to foreign and British territories.

William and the abolitionists within Parliament planned their strategy carefully. Since the bill was introduced by the government as a war measure, the abolitionist politicians agreed, as a ruse, to pay it little attention, drawing focus away from its real purpose. It felt odd to William to sit silently and watch other politicians push an anti-slave-trade bill. But the ruse worked perfectly. At the end of May 1806, the Foreign Slave Trade Abolition Bill was overwhelmingly passed into law.

On June 10, 1806, Charles Fox then offered a resolution to Parliament for the total abolition of the slave trade, declaring, "This House, conceiving the African slave trade to be contrary to the principles of justice, humanity, and sound policy, will, with all practicable expedition, proceed to take effectual measures for abolishing the said trade." Both chambers approved the resolution. William was delighted: the stage was now set for a bill abolishing the British slave trade. He wrote in his journal, "If it please God to spare the health of Fox, and to keep him and Grenville together, I hope we shall next year see the termination of all our labours."

Three weeks later Charles Fox fell ill, and by mid-September 1806 he had died. Without Fox's presence in the House of Commons, William wondered if they might be handed yet another defeat when the full anti-slave-trading bill was introduced to Parliament. He had been doing all he could to help the cause, including spending his summer vacation in Lyme Regis writing yet another pamphlet against the slave trade.

When William got back to London in the fall, he learned that Prime Minister William Grenville had decided to present the Abolition of the Slave Trade Bill to the House of Lords first, since getting such a bill passed in that chamber was always the sticking point. Once passed by the House of Lords, the bill would quickly be sent on to the House of Commons for a vote. Grenville had spent his summer urging the lords to vote for abolition. He showed William a list of seventy peers who had indicated they would vote for the measure, though he had no luck changing the opinions of the Duke of Clarence or the rest of the Royal Family.

With the passage of the Foreign Slave Trade Abolition Bill in May and its enforcement on the seas by the Royal Navy, one of the oldest arguments against abolishing the slave trade had fast faded from the scene. That argument was that if Great Britain gave up the trade, other nations would rush in to take her place. But that had not happened. In fact, Denmark had already banned the slave trade, and the United States was in the process of doing the same. Meanwhile France and Spain were blockaded and their ships unable to move freely around the globe, while Portugal did not have the resources to take over the slave trade for the British.

With the dawn of the New Year, it was time to present to Parliament the bill that would make Charles Fox's resolution of the year before the law of the land. William watched from the gallery on January 2, 1807, as the prime minister introduced the Abolition of the Slave Trade Bill into the House of Lords with a stirring speech. Following the bill's introduction, the Duke of Clarence managed to get debate on the measure delayed for a month. William was disappointed, but he was back in the gallery when debate on the bill opened on February 5 in the House of Lords.

During the debate the usual band of peers opposed the bill. As expected, the Duke of Clarence defended the slave trade, while Lord Westmorland aimed his attack squarely at William and his alliance with many Christian groups, saying, "Though I should see the Presbyterian and the prelate, the Methodist and the field preacher, the Jacobin and the murderer unite in support of it, in this House I will raise my voice against it." Thankfully, others in support of the measure drowned out Lord Westmorland, and the Abolition of the Slave Trade Bill passed the House of Lords by a vote of 100 for and 36 against.

The bill was sent on to the House of Commons, where, on February 23, its final reading and debate took place. William could hardly allow himself to believe that the fight might nearly be over. He took his seat in the House of Commons and listened to the debate. *The tide has turned. Thank God the tide has turned,* he said quietly to himself after each MP stood to argue for the abolition of the trade. Cheers rose each time William Wilberforce's name was mentioned. And when Sir Samuel Romilly rose and contrasted Napoleon's grasping for power with William's servant attitude, all the members of the House rose to their feet with deafening applause.

Such an outburst of emotion had never been seen in Parliament before. William put his face in his hands and wept. He told himself that surely now, at last, after two hundred years of cruelty, the slave trade was about to be banished from the British Empire. And it was. When the vote was taken, 283 members voted in favor of the Abolition of the Slave Trade Bill, while just 16 voted against it. Joy and relief washed over William.

Following the vote in the House of Commons, William retired with his friends to his home at 4 Old Palace Yard to celebrate. It was almost too much for William to take in. He had set out eighteen years before to get a bill banning the slave trade in the British Empire passed through Parliament, and now the task was complete. No longer would British ships be sailing into African harbors to pick up cargos of human slaves to be taken from their homeland to foreign shores to be worked to death.

William thought of his old friend John Newton, who was now eighty-one years old and ailing. Newton had lived long enough to see the slave trade, the thing he despised more than anything else, finally ended in Great Britain. William also thought of William Pitt. How he wished that his friend were alive to savor the moment with him!

For William, the passing of the Abolition of the Slave Trade Bill was just the first step in the grand scheme of ridding the world of slavery. He did not allow himself time to rest on his laurels. He still had much work ahead of him. Half a million slaves were still chained and whipped mercilessly to make them work in the British West Indies. Even though no one else from Africa could legally be forced to join them there, those slaves also deserved to be free.

Other groups of oppressed people also deserved freedom. William turned his attention to India, where girls and women and all those in the lowest castes of society, both women and men, suffered injustice. The British East India Company had a monopoly on trade with India and did not want anyone meddling in their business, especially telling them what they could or could not do with the local people. William knew from his contact with William Carey, the English Baptist missionary who made his home in Serampore, a Danish enclave in India, that conditions in British India were brutal. With no one to watch over them and no laws to prosecute them, some of the men of the East India Company were committing terrible crimes against poor Indians. William joined with a former governor-general of India in a campaign to have Parliament amend the charter of the East India Company so that missionaries and teachers would be allowed into the country to live and work.

With the passage of the anti-slave-trade bill behind him, William decided it was time to move his family into London. The Wilberforces moved to a large house at Kensington Gore, situated on three acres of land on the south side of Hyde Park. They moved in early 1808, soon after Barbara had given birth to their fourth son, Henry. William and Barbara now had four sons and two daughters. William Jr., their oldest child, was now nine years old. William and Barbara were concerned about him because he was strong-willed and more challenging to raise than all of the other children put together.

Although the Wilberforce family had lived at Clapham Common for ten years, William was not concerned about losing touch with all his friends there. In fact, being so close to Parliament made the Kensington Gore house busier than Broomfield Lodge had been.

One frequent visitor to the house was Spencer Perceval, the new prime minister. Grenville, who had resigned over the ongoing struggle over Catholic emancipation, had served as prime minister for only one year—the year that saw the abolition of the slave trade. Perceval then acted as chief minister during the second brief premiership of the Duke of Portland, who by now was too old and ill to govern. William liked Perceval, who formally became prime minister in 1809. He especially appreciated Perceval's views on India and the need to open the Indian subcontinent to British education and missionaries. Sadly, in May 1812 Perceval was shot to death in the lobby of the House of Commons. The assassin, a man named John Bellingham, had been trying to get an audience with the prime minister to discuss grievances over his imprisonment in Russia.

The country went into mourning following the assassination, and another election was called. For the first time since he had become one of the two Knights of the Shire for the County of Yorkshire twenty-eight years before, William seriously considered stepping down from his seat. He was now fifty-three years old and concerned that he wasn't home enough to guide his children as they grew up. Besides, William's constant attention on the anti-slave-trade bill had taken a toll on his body. He looked like a man of seventy. He was hunched from curvature of the spine and was becoming forgetful. Friends persuaded him not to step down completely from Parliament but rather to take up being the member for the pocket borough of Bramber. This would relieve him of a lot of the responsibility he bore in Parliament representing Yorkshire, the largest county in the country.

While Great Britain was still at war with France, in June 1812 the nation found itself in another war, this time with the United States. This war revolved around unresolved issues from the Revolutionary War and trade restrictions imposed by the ongoing war with France, the impressment of American merchant sailors into the Royal Navy, and British support of Indian tribes as a way to curb American expansion westward. Soon Great Britain had two armies fighting on two continents, putting further stress on the British economy.

The year 1812 also brought some good news in the war with the French. As they advanced into Russia, Napoleon and his army overstretched their supply lines. After making it all the way to Moscow, the onset of a severe Russian winter forced the French to retreat. Lacking food and fodder for the horses, the starving soldiers of the French army suffered greatly. Many died of hypothermia from the bitter cold, and throughout their retreat, the French were attacked by Russian troops, who were often joined in the fight by local peasants. By the time Napoleon made it out of Russia in late November, his army was nothing more than a remnant. In the attempted conquest of Russia, 380,000 of Napoleon's soldiers had died and another 100,000 had been taken prisoner. Only 27,000 soldiers managed to escape in the retreat from Russia.

William, like everyone else in Great Britain, was pleased with the news and hoped that it would hasten the end of the war with France. The people's hope increased when Napoleon's allies, Prussia and Austria, broke their alliance and switched sides in the war.

William's home remained a factory churning out good works. It seemed that William was asked to champion, or at least bless, every Christian or humanitarian reform effort during the next few years. William counted sixty-nine committees of which he was either the president, the vice president, or a member. Some of them, such as the British National Endeavor for the Orphans of Soldiers and Sailors, and the Society for the Bettering of Conditions and Increasing the Comforts of the Poor, dealt with large social issues, many of them caused or made worse by the long war with France. Others dealt with specific problems, such as the plight of the "climbing boys," boys as young as four years old who were forced to climb and clean the insides of chimneys. The boys routinely suffocated or were burned to death, and those who survived childhood often died of soot-related cancer before reaching adulthood.

Much to the delight of everyone in Great Britain, the year 1814 saw the tables turned on Napoleon when a coalition of troops from Russia, Austria, and Prussia invaded France and captured Paris at the end of March. Napoleon was forced to resign as emperor and was sent into exile on Elba, an island off the coast of Italy. It seemed to William that the protracted war with France was all but over.

The close of 1814 also brought a resolution to the war with the United States. The war had ground to a virtual stalemate, and peace between the two countries was finalized in the Treaty of Ghent, signed on December 24, 1814. The treaty went into effect in early 1815.

While 1815 opened with wars receding, William's year began with personal loss. On January 16, 1815, his friend and cousin Henry Thornton died of tuberculosis at the age of fifty-four. William was devastated. He recalled how as ten-year-old boys he and Henry had loved to explore the garden at Lauriston House and walk down to the Thames and watch ships sail by, how as bachelors they had lived together in the chummery at Clapham Common, and how Henry had been at his side in the anti-slave-trade battle. William would greatly miss Henry.

Just when it seemed things might be settling down on the European continent, the situation took a turn for the worse. William learned that Napoleon had escaped from exile on Elba and was riding through France raising a new army. It seemed there was still life left in the war with France after all. Things came to a head on June 18, 1815, in a battle fought near the town of Waterloo, just south of Brussels. The Duke of Wellington, leading an army made up of British, Dutch, and German troops, faced off against Napoleon and his army. When the battle was over, Napoleon had been defeated. When William heard the news, he was sure that this was the end. Sure enough, following his defeat, Napoleon resigned as the emperor of France for a second time. He surrendered to the British on July 15, when he was unable to find a way to flee France for the United States. Great Britain's long war with France ended on September 13, 1815. William hoped that the country could at last focus on repairing Britain's tattered economy.

A month after the end of the war with France, on October 12, Marianne Thornton died from the same illness that had claimed the life of her husband, Henry. She died leaving their nine children orphans. Almost exactly a year later, in October 1816, William's sister Sally became suddenly ill and died before he could rush to her side. It was hard for William to comprehend. He felt he was by far the sickliest member of his family, yet he had outlived all his siblings.

Despite the losses, William worked on. There was still a lot of good to be done, and if he was the sickliest of his family, he was living on borrowed time.

Late in 1816 William took his family to visit the Reverend Francis Cunningham and his wife, Richenda, at Pakefield on the east coast of England. He hoped for a quiet time away, or as quiet as possible, since he traveled with his wife, six children, two tutors, a private secretary, a lady's maid, a valet, and a nursemaid. As usual, news spread quickly that William Wilberforce was staying in the area, and visitors were soon arriving, seeking his help or patronage. One visitor was a man named Joseph John Gurney, who was Richenda Cunningham's brother. He asked William to accompany him back to his estate in Norwich to attend the annual meeting of the local British and Foreign Bible Society. Since William was on the national board of the society, they would be honored to have him at their local meeting. William agreed to go as long as Joseph John could accommodate his family and entourage. Joseph John agreed, and soon the Wilberforce family was ensconced at Earlham, the Gurney estate at Norwich, twenty-five miles north of Pakefield.

William was pleased with what he found at Earlham. Joseph John came from a large and industrious Quaker family. While staying at the estate, William also met Thomas Fowell Buxton, who was married to Joseph John's sister Hannah. William immediately liked Buxton, a successful businessman and an abolitionist. Buxton also was active in social reform, which led him to consider going into politics and perhaps becoming a member of the House of Commons. William encouraged him, since Parliament needed more able Christian members like Thomas Fowell Buxton.

For William, the reputation of another Gurney sister seemed to hang all over Earlham. Elizabeth Gurney Fry had grown up in the large house but now lived in London, where she was involved in prison reform. William had heard of her work among the women inmates at Newgate Prison and hoped that before too long he would get to meet her.

The visit to Earlham was a great success, and after attending the annual meeting of the local British and Foreign Bible Society, the Wilberforce family returned home. William was impressed with Joseph John's sincerity and thoughtful ways. Before leaving Norwich he invited him to come to London and visit at Kensington Gore.

Once back in London, William and Barbara had to decide what to do with their oldest son, William Jr., who was now eighteen years old and ready for college, or at least he should have been. However, William Jr. was not the studious type. He liked to follow racehorses and attend parties. William decided to send him to Trinity College, Cambridge, where he asked Isaac Milner to keep an eye on him. It was not enough. William was soon hearing disturbing stories about his oldest son's antics. He wrote many letters to William Jr., imploring him to study hard and pay attention to his tutors, something he was painfully aware he had not done himself when a student at Cambridge.

In early February 1818 William got to meet Elizabeth Fry in person and see firsthand her reform work at Newgate Prison. Barbara and two of her women friends accompanied William on the visit to Newgate. William was amazed at the polite behavior of the female prisoners. He had visited other prisons, where the inmates lived in deplorable conditions and were completely unmanageable. But in Newgate the women were kind and helpful to each other. A school had been set up to teach the children, and Elizabeth was constantly talking to the women about faith in

God and about what they would do with their lives when they got out of prison. William found Elizabeth warm and friendly and immediately became a supporter of her prison reform work.

William continued to hear bad reports about his son William Jr. At the beginning of 1819 he learned that his son had bought himself a second racehorse, despite William's telling him not to do so. That was the last straw. William withdrew William Jr. from Trinity College. He sent him to board with a friend in Harrow, where William Jr. met John Owen, the secretary of the local Bible Society. More important, William Jr. met John's daughter Mary, and the two fell in love and were quickly married.

On January 29, 1820, "mad" King George III died at the age of eighty-one, having reigned for nearly sixty years. His son, the Prince of Wales, who had been serving as regent since 1811, when his father's mental illness had returned, became King George IV.

By now the Wilberforces had moved out of London to a house in Godstone, Surrey, fifteen miles to the south. There were several reasons for the move. William had allowed his brother-in-law, Richard Spooner, to invest a lot of his money, much of which had been lost in bad investments. With his son William Jr. and a new daughter-in-law to support, along with three more sons to send to college, William needed to curb his expenses to save money. And living in the country was much cheaper than the city. Adding to William's stress was the fact that his older daughter, Barbara, was unwell, and he thought she might recover if they moved out of the city.

By 1821 William knew that he was not the man to carry forward the task of getting a bill through Parliament abolishing slavery in the British Empire. Like a relay runner, it was time for him to hand on the baton. As he looked around Parliament for a successor, William settled on a man he thought best suited to carry the abolition fight to its end—his new friend, Thomas Fowell Buxton, whom he had met at Earlham Estate in Norwich five years before. Buxton had been elected to the House of Commons as a member for Weymouth and Melcombe Regis and had proved himself an able politician. William decided to write to him and put the question of taking the lead in Parliament on the slave issue before him.

> I have for some time been viewing you in this connection . . . and can no longer forbear resorting to you . . . to take most seriously into consideration the expediency of your devoting yourself to this blessed service. . . . Let me then entreat you to form an alliance with me, that may truly be termed holy . . . ; and in forming a partnership of this sort with you, I cannot doubt that I should be doing an act highly pleasing to God, and beneficial to my fellow creatures.

Much to William's delight, Buxton accepted the invitation and became the new face of the antislavery movement in Parliament.

As 1821 drew to a close, William discovered he had been wrong about his daughter: being in the country had not helped her to get well. Like Henry and Marianne Thornton before her, twenty-two-year-old Barbara was suffering from tuberculosis, and she died from the disease on December 30.

A little over two years later, in 1824, William delivered yet another abolition speech in Parliament. Not long afterward he became ill. It took him a year to recover, and he knew it was time for him to retire from politics.

In February 1825, William sat in the House of Commons for the last time as a member of Parliament. He had spent forty-five years of his life in the Commons, doing what he could to alleviate suffering at home and abroad. Writing to a friend afterward, he confessed, "I always spoke and voted according to the dictates of my conscience, for the public and not for my own private interest. . . . Yet I am but too conscious of numerous and great sins of omission, many opportunities of doing good whether not at all or very inadequately improved."

Though retired from Parliament, William still had plenty to focus on.

Chapter 16

The Battle Won

There was no such word as *retire* in William Wilberforce's vocabulary. Even though he no longer sat in Parliament, William still attended hundreds of meetings and championed many of the same causes he had pursued all his political life. One organization he was pleased to be able to spend more time working with was the Society for the Prevention of Cruelty to Animals, or SPCA. William, along with Thomas Fowell Buxton, was one of a group of twenty-two reformers who had met at Old Slaughter's Coffee House in London the year before to start the SPCA.

William loved animals. At times his family had owned pet ponies, hares, dogs, cats, even turtles from the Caribbean islands. All around him, however, William saw evidence that many other people did not love animals in the same way. Many enjoyed sports that William believed to be nothing more than animal abuse. And he only had to walk down the street to see old horses being worked to death pulling heavy carts. When the horses fell over from exhaustion, their owners would unhitch them and leave them there.

Two years before, while still in Parliament, William had done all he could to help another MP, Irishman Richard Martin, push through the Ill Treatment of Cattle Bill. It was the first ever law to regulate cruelty to animals in Great Britain. After passage of the bill, William realized that much more needed to be done to curb cruelty to animals. He was confident that the SPCA would grow into a large and powerful organization that would help animals and, just as important, make people behave in more humane ways toward them.

Many of the organizations William helped to found and fund were flourishing. He was particularly pleased with the British and Foreign Bible Society. In the twenty years since the society had started in response to Mary Jones's search for a Welsh Bible, it had distributed over four million Bibles. The society had also translated the Bible into 140 languages. As a result, William received letters of thanks from missionaries around the world.

The year after William retired from Parliament, he and Barbara moved to a farm called Highwood Hill. William Jr., his wife, Mary, and their son, William, soon joined them at the farm. William was concerned for his oldest son. The other three boys, Robert, Samuel, and Henry, were all now hard-working young scholars. They attended Oxford University and had found their own Christian faith. In fact, all three were studying to become clergymen, but not William Jr., who was constantly looking for a quick way to get rich.

Since William Jr. had not gone back to college, William and Barbara wanted to help him find a career. They listened as their son worked hard to convince them that he could make a good living as a farmer or, more precisely, as a dairyman, raising cows and selling their milk to London. William sold most of his stock and even the family house he had inherited at Hull and loaned the money to his oldest son. But by 1830 William Jr. had lost it all and more, and had fled to Switzerland with his family to avoid the debt.

To clear his son's debts of over fifty thousand pounds so that William Jr. and his family could return to England, William sold the Highwood Hill farm and pensioned off his faithful servants. As astonishing as it was to seventy-year-old William, he was no longer a wealthy man. Yet, as always, he found cause to thank God for this unexpected turn in old age. William wrote to a friend,

> Mrs. Wilberforce and I are supplied with a delightful asylum under the roofs of two of our own children [Samuel and Robert] and what better could we desire? A kind Providence has enabled me with truth to adopt the declaration of David, that goodness and mercy have followed me all my days. . . . I cannot understand why my life has been spared so long, except it be to show that a man can be as happy without a fortune as with one.

Sadly, William's old age was marred by another family tragedy. In January 1831 his surviving daughter, Elizabeth, married a poor minister named John James. The couple set up home in the industrial town of Rawmarsh in Yorkshire. Shortly after giving birth to a daughter, who was named Barbara, Elizabeth developed a lung infection and soon died. She was thirty-one years old and had been married little more than a year.

On April 12, 1832, a month after Elizabeth's death, William signed his name to a petition to end slavery in all of Great Britain's colonies. This fight to completely end slavery had been long and difficult. Thomas Fowell Buxton had brought repeated bills before Parliament, but each met the same opposition and delays as the bills William had brought year after year to end the slave trade.

During Christmas 1831, however, a large-scale slave revolt had broken out in Jamaica, and it turned the tide in favor of complete abolition. After the slave revolt was put down, the British government sent officials to Jamaica to investigate the loss of property and lives. The findings of these inquiries once again reminded the British people of the deplorable and inhumane condition slaves were forced to live under in many of their colonies.

In response to this, during 1832 the antislavery movement geared up for another attempt to pass an antislavery bill in Parliament. This time the bill included a clause that would allow the British government to pay twenty million pounds to slave owners as compensation for forcing them to free their slaves. This was a huge sum of money—about 40 percent of the total amount the government spent in a year. Many people thought the slave owners should not be paid any money at all for freeing their slaves, but William thought it a small price to pay to finally rid the British Empire of the scourge of slavery.

By now many of the sons of the old guard in the fight to end the slave trade were on the front lines of the total abolition battle, including the sons of William's brother-in-law James Stephen, James Jr. and George Stephen. James Jr. was now a lawyer and government advisor to the board of trade. He had drawn up the wording for the new parliamentary bill. His brother George, a brilliant young solicitor, argued for the payment of compensation to the slave owners. Thomas Babington Macaulay, an MP for Leeds and the eldest son of Zachary Macaulay, the former governor of Sierra Leone for the Sierra Leone Company, also was a strong supporter of abolition.

As the general election of 1832 approached, these new fighters managed to make abolition a central theme of the election. They went directly to voters and urged them to vote only for candidates who promised to vote for the end of slavery. To inform voters, they published tables showing which candidates were for or against ending slavery and which had not declared their intentions.

During the summer, William's second son, Robert, married Agnes Wrangham, the daughter of an archdeacon. The newlyweds moved into the vicarage at East Farleigh and invited William and Barbara to live with them. The vicarage was just one mile from

Barham Court, where the Middletons had lived and from where, nearly fifty years before, Sir Charles Middleton had written to William and asked him to take up the antislavery fight in Parliament.

By now William, his body held upright by an iron-and-leather frame worn under his shirt, was too frail to walk and had to be pushed around in a wheelchair. But his spirits remained bright, and his failing eyes, as always, were fixed firmly on the prize of abolition.

In Maidstone, Kent, on April 12, 1833, William found the strength to make one last speech in support of the abolition of slavery. He spoke briefly, and as a beam of sunlight shone in through the window, he ended with the statement, "The object is bright before us. The light of heaven beams upon it and is an earnest [a sign] of success."

A week later William and Barbara set out to stay with their son Samuel in Brighstone on the Isle of Wight. On the way William caught influenza, and he and Barbara diverted to Bath so that William could "take the waters," as he had so many times before.

The treatment in Bath helped William a little, though his legs swelled up and he spent hours resting on a sofa. He told those who inquired about how he was doing that he felt like a "clock which is almost run down." But he clung on. In mid-May 1833 William received the news he had eagerly awaited for two-thirds of his life. The Abolition of Slavery Bill, the bill that everyone believed would pass this time, had been introduced into Parliament. William received the news in a letter from his old fellow abolitionist friend Zachary Macaulay. The letter was dated May 15, 1833.

> My dear friend,
>
> This day ten years ago the abolition of slavery was first made a question in Parliament. Last night its death-blow was struck. I send you a copy of the debate. Stanley's allusion to you was quite overpowering, and electrified the House. My dear friend, let me unite with you in thanks to God for this mercy.

In July, William was still ill, and his family decided he should go to London to see Dr. Chambers. In London, William and Barbara stayed with William's cousin Lucy Smith.

On Friday, July 26, 1833, a month before William Wilberforce's seventy-fourth birthday, the Abolition of Slavery Bill passed its second reading in the House of Commons and was sent on to the House of Lords for a vote, where its passage was assured of success. When William heard the news, he was overcome with emotion. The fight was over, the battle won! William thanked God that he had lived long enough to see it. Three days later in London, on July 29, 1833, William Wilberforce died quietly, his wife at his side.

The following day the Lord Chancellor asked William's sons to allow their father's body to be buried at Westminster Abbey, next to his friend William Pitt. It was a great national honor. On Saturday, August

3, 1833, Parliament closed for the funeral. Throngs of people lined the streets of London as Great Britain mourned the passing of an elder statesman and humble politician. The 800,000 slaves in the West Indies had yet to hear the dual news of their freedom and of the death of the man who had made it his life's work to gain their liberty.

The Slavery Abolition Act was passed by the House of Lords and given Royal Assent on August 28, 1833, becoming the law of the land. As the bill decreed, on August 1, 1834, all slaves in British colonies were set free and slavery became illegal throughout the empire.

Bibliography

Baehr, Ted, Susan Wales, and Ken Wales. *Amazing Grace of Freedom: The Inspiring Faith of William Wilberforce, the Slaves' Champion.* Green Forest, AR: New Leaf Press, 2007.

Belmonte, Kevin. *William Wilberforce: A Hero for Humanity.* Grand Rapids: Zondervan, 2007.

Furneaux, Robin. *William Wilberforce.* London: Hamilton, 1974.

Lean, Garth. *God's Politician: William Wilberforce's Struggle to Abolish the Slave Trade and Reform the Morals of a Nation.* Colorado Springs: Helmers & Howard, 1987.

Metaxas, Eric. *Amazing Grace: William Wilberforce and the Heroic Campaign to End Slavery.* New York: HarperOne, 2007.

Pollock, John. *Wilberforce: God's Statesman.* Eastbourne, UK: Kingsway, 1977.

Stott, Anne. *Wilberforce: Family and Friends.* New York: Oxford University Press, 2012.

About the Authors

Janet and Geoff Benge are a husband and wife writing team with more than thirty years of writing experience. Janet is a former elementary school teacher. Geoff holds a degree in history. Together they have a passion to make history come alive for a new generation of readers.

Originally from New Zealand, the Benges make their home in the Orlando, Florida, area.

HEROES OF HISTORY are available in paperback, e-book, and audiobook formats, with more titles coming soon! Curriculum Guides are also available for all U.S. biographies.

www.heroesofhistory.com

Also from Janet and Geoff Benge...

More adventure-filled biographies for ages 10 to 100!

Christian Heroes: Then and Now

Gladys Aylward: The Adventure of a Lifetime • 978-1-57658-019-6
Nate Saint: On a Wing and a Prayer • 978-1-57658-017-2
Hudson Taylor: Deep in the Heart of China • 978-1-57658-016-5
Amy Carmichael: Rescuer of Precious Gems • 978-1-57658-018-9
Eric Liddell: Something Greater Than Gold • 978-1-57658-137-7
Corrie ten Boom: Keeper of the Angels' Den • 978-1-57658-136-0
William Carey: Obliged to Go • 978-1-57658-147-6
George Müller: Guardian of Bristol's Orphans • 978-1-57658-145-2
Jim Elliot: One Great Purpose • 978-1-57658-146-9
Mary Slessor: Forward into Calabar • 978-1-57658-148-3
David Livingstone: Africa's Trailblazer • 978-1-57658-153-7
Betty Greene: Wings to Serve • 978-1-57658-152-0
Adoniram Judson: Bound for Burma • 978-1-57658-161-2
Cameron Townsend: Good News in Every Language • 978-1-57658-164-3
Jonathan Goforth: An Open Door in China • 978-1-57658-174-2
Lottie Moon: Giving Her All for China • 978-1-57658-188-9
John Williams: Messenger of Peace • 978-1-57658-256-5
William Booth: Soup, Soap, and Salvation • 978-1-57658-258-9
Rowland Bingham: Into Africa's Interior • 978-1-57658-282-4
Ida Scudder: Healing Bodies, Touching Hearts • 978-1-57658-285-5
Wilfred Grenfell: Fisher of Men • 978-1-57658-292-3
Lillian Trasher: The Greatest Wonder in Egypt • 978-1-57658-305-0
Loren Cunningham: Into All the World • 978-1-57658-199-5
Florence Young: Mission Accomplished • 978-1-57658-313-5
Sundar Singh: Footprints Over the Mountains • 978-1-57658-318-0
C.T. Studd: No Retreat • 978-1-57658-288-6
Rachel Saint: A Star in the Jungle • 978-1-57658-337-1
Brother Andrew: God's Secret Agent • 978-1-57658-355-5
Clarence Jones: Mr. Radio • 978-1-57658-343-2
Count Zinzendorf: Firstfruit • 978-1-57658-262-6
John Wesley: The World His Parish • 978-1-57658-382-1
C. S. Lewis: Master Storyteller • 978-1-57658-385-2
David Bussau: Facing the World Head-on • 978-1-57658-415-6
Jacob DeShazer: Forgive Your Enemies • 978-1-57658-475-0
Isobel Kuhn: On the Roof of the World • 978-1-57658-497-2
Elisabeth Elliot: Joyful Surrender • 978-1-57658-513-9
D. L. Moody: Bringing Souls to Christ • 978-1-57658-552-8
Paul Brand: Helping Hands • 978-1-57658-536-8
Dietrich Bonhoeffer: In the Midst of Wickedness • 978-1-57658-713-3
Francis Asbury: Circuit Rider • 978-1-57658-737-9
Samuel Zwemer: The Burden of Arabia • 978-1-57658-738-6

Klaus-Dieter John: Hope in the Land of the Incas • 978-1-57658-826-2
Mildred Cable: Through the Jade Gate • 978-1-57658-886-4
John Flynn: Into the Never Never • 978-1-57658-898-7
Richard Wurmbrand: Love Your Enemies • 978-1-57658-987-8
Charles Mulli: We Are Family • 978-1-57658-894-9
John Newton: Change of Heart • 978-1-57658-909-0
Helen Roseveare: Mama Luka • 978-1-57658-910-6
Norman Grubb: Mission Builder • 978-1-57658-915-1
Albert Schweitzer: Le Grand Docteur • 978-1-57658-961-8

Heroes of History

George Washington Carver: From Slave to Scientist • 978-1-883002-78-7
Abraham Lincoln: A New Birth of Freedom • 978-1-883002-79-4
Meriwether Lewis: Off the Edge of the Map • 978-1-883002-80-0
George Washington: True Patriot • 978-1-883002-81-7
William Penn: Liberty and Justice for All • 978-1-883002-82-4
Harriet Tubman: Freedombound • 978-1-883002-90-9
John Adams: Independence Forever • 978-1-883002-50-3
Clara Barton: Courage under Fire • 978-1-883002-51-0
Daniel Boone: Frontiersman • 978-1-932096-09-5
Theodore Roosevelt: An American Original • 978-1-932096-10-1
Douglas MacArthur: What Greater Honor • 978-1-932096-15-6
Benjamin Franklin: Live Wire • 978-1-932096-14-9
Christopher Columbus: Across the Ocean Sea • 978-1-932096-23-1
Laura Ingalls Wilder: A Storybook Life • 978-1-932096-32-3
Orville Wright: The Flyer • 978-1-932096-34-7
Captain John Smith: A Foothold in the New World • 978-1-932096-36-1
Thomas Edison: Inspiration and Hard Work • 978-1-932096-37-8
Alan Shepard: Higher and Faster • 978-1-932096-41-5
Ronald Reagan: Destiny at His Side • 978-1-932096-65-1
Davy Crockett: Ever Westward • 978-1-932096-67-5
Milton Hershey: More Than Chocolate • 978-1-932096-82-8
Billy Graham: America's Pastor • 978-1-62486-024-9
Ben Carson: A Chance at Life • 978-1-62486-034-8
Louis Zamperini: Redemption • 978-1-62486-049-2
Elizabeth Fry: Angel of Newgate • 978-1-62486-064-5
William Wilberforce: Take Up the Fight • 978-1-62486-057-7
William Bradford: Plymouth's Rock • 978-1-62486-092-8
Ernest Shackleton: Going South • 978-1-62486-093-5
Benjamin Rush: The Common Good • 978-1-62486-123-9
Dwight Eisenhower: Supreme Commander • 978-1-62486-142-0
Frederick Douglass: The Right to Dignity • 978-1-62486-151-2
Winston Churchill: Resolute • 978-1-62486-153-6